Knowing Jesus
Lessons in the Gospel of John
(Volume I)

© By Dr. Randall D. Smith

"Scripture quotations taken from the New American Standard Bible®,
Copyright © 1960, 1962, 1963, 1968, 1971, 1972, 1973,
1975, 1977, 1995 by The Lockman Foundation
Used by permission." (www.Lockman.org)

These volumes were prepared with students and teachers of the Bible in mind. The series is taken from the actual teaching notes of Dr. Smith as he teaches through all of the Bible each year at Great Commission Bible Institute in Sebring, Florida.

Knowing Jesus
Lessons in the Gospel of John

Table of Contents

Table of Contents 3

Lesson One: John 1:1-18 "The Invasion of God" 5

Lesson Two: John 1:19-51 "The Big Five" 15

Lesson Three: John 2:1-25 "The Surprising Savior" 25

Lesson Four: John 3:1-21 "The Total Makeover" 35

Lesson Five: John 3:22-36 "Father Loves Most" 49

Lesson Six: John 4:1-54 "I Object!" 59

Lesson Seven: John 4:27-42 "The 'Wax On, Wax Off' Discipleship School" 73

Lesson Eight: John 4:46-54 "Long Distance Healing" 87

Lesson Nine: John 5: 1-47 "How to Start a Religion and Kill Real Faith" 97

Lesson Ten: John 6:1-71 "Eating is Believing - Six Principles of Real Fulfillment" 105

Lesson 11: John 7:1-53 "Six Places the Truth Cannot Be Found!" 115

Lesson Twelve: John 8:1-20 "The 'Do Over' Grace of God" 127

Knowing Jesus 139

Lesson Thirteen: John 8:12-59 "Show Me Something *Real*!" 139

Lesson Fourteen: John 9:1-41 "I Can See Clearly Now!" 149

Lesson Fifteen: John 10:1-21 "Ultimate Security" 161

Lesson Sixteen: John 10:22-42 "Hearing God" 175

Lesson Seventeen: John 11:1- 46 "Night Vision" 183

Lesson Eighteen: John 11:47-57 "The Titanic Choice"……………189

Knowing Jesus
Lessons in the Gospel of John

Lesson One: John 1:1-18 "The Invasion of God"

After four hurricanes ripped across the Florida Peninsula, Floridians began to appreciate the awesome force of the storms and the incredible privilege of electric power. When the power lines snapped, the connection to important everyday concepts like lighted rooms, cool homes, fresh, crisp vegetables – all took on a new meaning. The point was clear – connection broken equals darkness. The fact that the generator could MAKE the power was not helpful, unless there was a line to DELIVER the power.

I am living in a time when people think we can have the benefits of the power without the connections.

A recent study showed that a significant percentage of Americans were finding God. One *NY Times* editorial commentator (Charles Blow) was horrified and lamented: So what was the reason for this flight of the unchurched to churches? Did God appear in a bush? Did the grass look greener on the other side of the cross? Or was it a response to the social pressure of being nonreligious in a very Christian country? None of those reasons topped the list. Most said that they first joined a religion because their spiritual needs were not being met. And the most-cited reason for settling on their current religion was that they simply enjoyed the services and style of worship. For these newly converted, the nonreligious shtick didn't stick. There was still a void, and communities of the faithful helped fill it. While science, logic and reason are on the side of the nonreligious, the cold, hard facts are just so cold and hard. Yes, the evidence for evolution is irrefutable. Yes, there is a plethora of biblical contradictions. Yes, there is mounting evidence from neuroscientists that suggests that God may be a product of the mind. Yes, yes, yes. But when is the choir going to sing? And when is the picnic? And is my child going to get a part in the holiday play? As the nonreligious movement picks up steam, it needs do a better job of appealing to the ethereal part of our human exceptionalism — that wondrous, precious part where logic and reason hold little purchase, where love and compassion reign. It's the part that fears loneliness, craves companionship and needs affirmation and fellowship. We are more than cells, synapses and sex drives. We are amazing, mysterious creatures forever in search of something greater than ourselves.

My question is: Why would you believe that man is anything more special than a complicated DNA string of what could be considered a higher form of virus?

The world persists with the claim that we follow "cleverly devised myths." Jesus was a fake and there is no God. When we die, there is nothing else. God is a creation of the human mind. A hapless accident caused the world you see below and the heavens in their expanse above. Planets spin and whirl according to no particular design. The delicate web of cells makes the flowers of the field – all a cosmic fluke. There is no plan. There is no future. Man is an animal among the evolved DNA strands of the universe… yet you should behave. You should do things to benefit others. You should care about how poor and suffering people live. You should try to keep the planet green. We should advance the knowledge of the species. We should live well and seek a meaningful life where – we essentially agree - there is none. Why?

The unbeliever offers a sad picture, but without a personal experience with God it is not hard to understand. One cannot see God by looking at RELIGION. In fact, religion more illustrates man's hard heart and ego-filled soul than the goodness of God. In the name of religion, wars rage across the planet. One cannot see God by looking at MORALITY and CONSCIENCE, for these change with the tide of public opinion in the age. To really understand God, you must MEET Him and have His eyes pierce your heart.

How do I know? Enter God's Word. Open the Bible. The Bible is not silent on God, His Word, or His testimony.

2 Peter 1:16 For we did not follow cleverly devised tales when we made known to you the power and coming of our Lord Jesus Christ, but we were eyewitnesses of His majesty...21 for no prophecy was ever made by an act of human will, but men moved by the Holy Spirit spoke from God.

2 Timothy 3:16 All Scripture is inspired by God and profitable for teaching, for reproof, for correction, for training in righteousness.

Now zero in on John's Gospel. John wrote that "One day, God invaded the planet!" Hebrews 1 says that God sent prophets, but felt the best way to reach man was to have His Son put on skin. Philippians 2 says Jesus chose to do the work from Heaven's throne.

Philippians 2:6 Who, although He existed in the form of God, did not regard equality with God a thing to be grasped, 7 but emptied Himself, taking the form of a bond-servant, and being made in the likeness of men.

Key Principle: Jesus came to show the fullness of the Father and offer a renewed connection to men that would acknowledge Him.

John opens the Gospel with an **introduction of Jesus.**

The Purpose of Jesus' ministry on Earth.

Focus on the identity of the subject in the word "**WORD**."

What is a word?

- It is a collection of sounds to convey a truth.
- It is an expression of thought from one to another.
- It is the basic building block of communication – a thought expressed.

How do we know the "word" here is Jesus? Compare this with 1:14-15 and John the Baptizer's message. It is clear who the writer is speaking about. Jesus is the very expression of Who God is – so He is called the Word (1:1a). In Revelation 1:8, Jesus declared that He is the complete thought of Who God is. He said, "I am the "Alpha and Omega," the beginning and the end. He is God's Word, but also God's complete alphabet, the One Who spells out DEITY for us. Jesus makes the incomprehensible God able to be grasped and held close.

There is an amazing piece of art done by a Korean artist named Elder Rhee which is unique. It took him two years to complete the scroll. The artist meticulously drew the picture by hand with a very fine-tipped pen. It is not a painting, but a picture created by writing thousands of words with shaded letters. It is actually the entire New Testament written out by hand. There are about 185,000 words on the scroll with an average of a thousand words per line. The letters are drawn, some thick and some thin, so that they bring out a picture of Christ. There are twenty-seven angels surrounding Christ and looking to him, representing the twenty-seven books of the New Testament. The original work was six feet long by four feet wide. The figure of Christ is not imposed onto the words; the words reveal the picture of Christ as they are inked light and dark to bring out the portrait of Christ. The words have become flesh, a person. If you would magnify a portion of the work, such as Christ's hand, you could actually read the words. The message of the artist is that the New

Testament reveals one thing — the person of Jesus Christ. (Pastor Rod Buchanon, sermon central)

The Position of Jesus before He came.

Jesus was present with God the Father (Whose name is "The Ever Present One") and was in One in essence with Him (1:1-2). The "Word was with God," indicates that Jesus Christ existed in a face-to-face relationship with the Father.

Four questions should be examined before we move on:

- **Who exactly was Jesus according to the Bible?** The Christian Scriptures teach that Jesus is the very eternal God that deliberately chose to put on human skin. He is both God and Savior (Titus 2:13), Who was the agent of Creation (Gen. 1:1; Col.1:16-17) called God at that time. He was conscious before His birth as a baby in Bethlehem, and deliberately chose to come as Savior (Phil. 2:6). He always was the Eternal Son of God, and did NOT BECOME the Son of God AFTER Bethlehem or Calvary. He said in John 8:58: "<u>Before</u> Abraham was born, I am."

- **Why is He called SON?** He is the "Son" in personality (One Who serves the purpose of His Father, yet is singular in <u>essence</u> and <u>position</u>). The term "Son" does not imply inferiority of person, merely function. If one holds that, it makes Him "less" as a wife is less than her husband, for the two are compared in 1 Corinthians 11:3.

- **Do the Gospels claim Jesus was actually God on Earth?** In the Gospels, Jewish leaders recognized that Jesus personally calling God His Own Father was reason to kill Him (John 5:17-18) as it was blasphemy. They clearly saw Him claiming a divine nature (John 10:33). Note that in John 10:36 the indication is that the term "Son of God" was openly called blasphemy. In other words, the term "Son of God" was claiming to be essentially one in essence with God. In John 15:19-21, 25-26 Jesus claimed to have God's powers and do what God alone can do. In John 5:23 Jesus claimed that He was to be honored as God is honored. A very clear instance of what the disciples taught is found in John 20:28 in the mouth of Thomas: "My Lord and My God!" (If Thomas was simply "surprised" as some have argued, Jesus was required by law to be obedient to Exodus 20:7 and rebuke His disciple for the vain use of God's name in error!). He should have done what the Pharisees did in the Garden of Gethsemane, fell back and torn His clothing (John 18:6) when Jesus called Himself the "I Am." The record of the Gospels is clear – the disciples believed Jesus was not just the Savior from God, nor the Son from God – but God Who came to save!

- **Do the Epistles claim Jesus was actually God on Earth?**
In the writings of the Apostles the term "only begotten" is used to denote the difference between Jesus as the Divine Son and other believers that are also sons (Rom. 8:14) and begotten (John 1:13; 1 John 3:9, 4:7, 5:1,4,18). We as believers partake in God's divine nature in part (2 Peter 1:4) but do not have its fullness, alone found in the eternal Son of God. To be sure, in the testimony of Hebrews 1, the Father in Heaven ascribes deity to the Son in Hebrews 1:8-9. In both statements of the two verses, the Father called the Son "GOD." Scripture refers to the incarnate Messiah as both the Son of God and Son of Man. "Son of man" denotes true humanity, and "Son of God" does the same for His deity - linguistically they function in the same way. Hebrews 1:2 indicates the Son was the specific agent of creation of the world, that which was attributed to God in Genesis 1. Only God can create out of nothing. Further, Hebrews 1:2-3 assert that as the Son, the Shekinah of God shone - something only ascribed to God in the scriptures. The text declares that Jesus is the "exact representation" of the Father.

The Power of Jesus

- **Jesus was the singular agent of the Creation of PHYSICAL life** (1:3; cp. Genesis 1:1; Colossians 1:16-17). There was no other creator and no other helper. Everything that was made was made exclusively by Him.

- **Jesus was the author of SPIRITUAL life** – the life that illuminated men's hearts and connection with the Living God (1:4). Spiritual darkness spilled into our world in Genesis 3 and can only be removed by the Lord who is life and light. That life connection to God cord was snapped in death in the Garden of Eden, causing those who were dead to have no comprehension of the light when He stood before them (1:5). They didn't comprehend Him in His presence for the same reason they don't comprehend Him now - the world has no hunger for a LORD and MASTER.

The Presentation of Jesus

- **Jesus was made known to us** by John the prophet who was sent by God with an entire message that was to point people to Jesus (1:6-8).

- **The presentation was historical**: John came (1:6) and Jesus (The Word) came (1:14).

What other religion do you know whose God comes in person to die for his people? Buddha did not claim to be God, nor did he claim to have come from God. He was in search of the divine principle — the word become word. And neither did Mohammed claim to be God, only a prophet of God and author of the Koran. In all of the other world religions we have the word become word — a verbal revelation: writings, injunctions and moral codes. Only in Christianity does the Word become flesh.

- **The presentation was purposed**: He was sent from God as a witness to testify of the connection to God (light - 1:6-8)

Max Lucado tells the story about a tribe of people who lived in a dark, cold cave. The cave dwellers would huddle together and cry against the chill. Loud and long they wailed. It was all they did. It was all they knew to do. The sounds in the cave were mournful, but the people didn't know it, for they had never known joy. The spirit in the cave was death, but the people didn't know it, for they had never known life. But one day they heard a different voice. "I have heard your cries," it announced. "I have felt your chill and seen your darkness. I have come to help you." The cave people grew quiet. They had never heard this voice. Hope sounded strange to their ears. "How can we know you have come to help?" "Trust me," he answered. "I have what you need." The cave people peered through the darkness at the figure of the stranger. He was stacking something, then stooping and stacking more. "What are you doing?" one cried, nervously. The stranger didn't answer. "What are you making?" another shouted even louder. There was still no response. "Tell us!" demanded a third. The visitor stood and spoke in the direction of the voices. "I have what you need." With that he turned to the pile at his feet and lit it. Wood ignited, flames erupted, and light filled the cavern. The people turned away in fear. "Put it out!" they cried. "It hurts to see it." "Light always hurts before it helps," he answered. "Step closer. The pain will soon pass." "Not I," declared a voice. "Nor I," agreed a second. "Only a fool would risk exposing his eyes to such light," said another. The stranger stood next to the fire. "Would you prefer the darkness? Would you prefer the cold? Don't consult your fears. Take a step of faith." For a long time no one spoke. The people hovered in groups covering their eyes. The fire builder stood next to the fire. "It's warm here," he invited. "He's right," one from behind him announced. "It is warmer." The stranger turned to see a figure slowly stepping toward the fire. "I can open my eyes now," she proclaimed. "I can see." "Come closer," invited the fire builder. She did. She stepped into the ring of light. "It's so warm!" She extended her hands and sighed as her chill began to pass. "Come, everyone! Feel the warmth," she invited. "Silence woman!" cried one of the cave dwellers. "Dare you lead us into your folly? Leave us. Leave us and take your light with you." She turned to the stranger. "Why won't they come?" "They choose the chill, for though it's cold, it's what they know. They'd rather be cold than to change." "And live in the dark?" she asked. "And live in the dark," he replied.

• **The presentation was conclusive:** He identified the light as TRUE (1:9a)

• **The presentation was divisive:** The Word was able to connect every man – but they needed to recognize Him (1:9b-11); When He reconnected them they became children of God (1:12-13). Failure to do so would leave them in the darkness and disconnected.

2 Corinthians 5:21 He made Him Who knew no sin to be sin on our behalf, so that we might become the righteousness of God in Him.

• **The presentation was personal:** John publicly pointed to Jesus as the One (1:15), the complete revelation (1:16-17).

• **The presentation was clear:** Jesus gave a full, complete and accurate rendering of Who God is and how man can have a relationship with Him.

On March 5, 1994, Deputy Sheriff Lloyd Prescott was teaching a class for police officers in the Salt Lake City Library. During a break he stepped into the hallway, and as he did he saw a gunman forcing 18 hostages into a nearby room. Prescott, who was dressed in street clothes, fell in line with the group and became the nineteenth hostage. The gunman had not noticed him, and Prescott followed them into the room, and shut the door. The gunman announced the order in which hostages would be executed, and then it was that Prescott identified himself as a police officer. A fight ensued, and Prescott, in self-defense, shot the gunman. All of the hostages were released unharmed. The officer placed himself at great risk, but he was not thinking of himself, he was thinking about the danger the hostages were in.

An Anglican pastor wrote: In my former parish, my colleague once told the story of a young man who was mentally challenged, and always dreamed of participating in the Christmas pageant. Let's call him Robert. Every year Robert was overlooked for a speaking part in the pageant for fear that he would forget his lines. Finally one year, the pageant director decided to give Robert a speaking part. He was the innkeeper and his words were, "There is no room for you at the inn." Robert practiced his lines over and over. At last, the evening of the pageant came and a weary looking Mary and Joseph approached the door of the inn. The entire congregation held its breath when it came time for Robert to deliver his lines, and he said them excellently. However, as Mary and Joseph turned to leave and were almost halfway down the aisle, there was a look of consternation on Robert's face, and the pageant director held her breath because she knew that something was about to happen. Robert ran up to the couple and said in a loud voice so that everyone could hear, "Wait a minute. Come back. You can have my room." Robert opened his heart in the same way God opened God's heart to us through the birth of Jesus then, and continues to open God's heart to us, now. This, my friends, is the never-ending story. Do you have room?

Remember, Jesus came to show the fullness of the Father and offer a renewed connection to men that would acknowledge Him.

Knowing Jesus
Lessons in the Gospel of John

Lesson Two: John 1:19-51 "The Big Five"

Among psychologists, the phrase "Big Five" refers to five broad factors of personality - theoretically discerned and then rated for comparison by testing a subject. First mentioned in 1933, the five factors are Openness, Conscientiousness, Extraversion, Agreeableness, and Neuroticism (OCEAN, or CANOE if rearranged).

In our text, the "**big five**" refers to **five men** (Andrew, John the Disciple, Simon Peter, Philip and Nathaniel) that came to Jesus through the preaching of John the Baptizer. Like the "big five" psychological personalities, all five of these men were **unique**. They didn't **come** to Jesus the same way, because God reaches different people different ways for different purposes!

I want to take a simple approach to some observations about their lives as revealed by the Spirit in John 1. In the text I see **FIVE OBSERVATIONS ON GOD'S TRANSFORMATION WORK IN US** – another "big five" if you will.

Before we jump in to the five observations, I want to offer a few words that I hope will penetrate our hearts…

I have been a believer for a long time. I have spent time in half a dozen churches both on staff and in the chairs where you are. I have heard many a message on outreach and evangelism. I have been door to door in communities. I have shared Christ across a dining room table, in a train station, on an airplane, in a horse stable and over a dead body. I have stood before large numbers and proclaimed Jesus as Lord, and I have sat while a young man sobbed and gave his heart to the Lord…. and I am concerned today.

I am concerned because a great many preach and share Christ out of a sense of duty. Others share Christ out of fear that we are losing ground to a pagan culture. Some, I dare say, share Christ out of greed for money and lust for power. They want more people to come to their church and help them feel more significant... I am hearing fewer and fewer that are sharing out of brokenness for the lost world. Jesus taught that even something as holy looking as prayer can be used as a show ... Our compulsion for importance and significance opens our hearts to a legion of sinful attitudes and actions.

We cannot truly reach people we do not care about – and today care is getting harder to find. We are very busy, so very busy. Can we see them anymore? We lose our Father's heart when we don't see the world through our Father's eyes...

Key Principle: When we understand what God is doing in the people around us, we will see them as He sees them.

Observation 1: Some believers are called to prepare and equip others both in pre-evangelism and early disciple training.

For this, let's take a few moments to look carefully at **the call and ministry of John the Baptizer**, the cousin of Jesus in John 1:19-34.

> First, John lived out a testimony that invited questions by people (1:19). Here is one of the great truths about outreach: We must live in such a way that others see something in us they must know more about!
>
> Second, John deliberately turned any focus on HIM to focus on Messiah – this is NOT ABOUT ME (1:20-23). Another great truth: We must live in such a way that others are directed to Jesus through our lives and lips. We cannot lead them to our talents, our purity, our decency. Short of an

encounter with Jesus, they have failed to reach the destination necessary for every man's heart!

Third, John knew his **work** was attracting the attention, but his **words** were the heart of all that he should accomplish (1:24-28). The truth: We need to care for people and offer real help to those around us. Our work cannot be just talk. At the same time, living a good life and caring for others will not bring them to Jesus. We must work, but we must witness. Out of balance in words and we become preachers with no substance. Out of balance with works and we become empty philanthropists.

Fourth, John shared with people the **progression** of his own transformation by Jesus (1:29-34). John spoke openly of three areas:

- **Identity**: He began with Jesus being the substitute for all of our sins, and the Lord above us all (1:29-30).

- **Personal Journey**: He honestly shared that he had missed the truth of Who Jesus is (1:31a) and as a result he changed his lifestyle to draw attention to the truth he found in Jesus (1:31b)!!

- **Work**: He made sure that the work of Jesus was his central message (1:32-34). Jesus was approved of God (32), empowered by God (33), and the eternal Son of God (34).

Truth: God hasn't left us with nothing to share. People need to know that God sent His Son, and that Son was empowered to care for man's need. Apart from that message, we have no hope. We cannot earn God's love, for we stand condemned -- whether claiming ignorance, independent morality or religiosity (Rom. 1:1-3:20). Yet God was rich in mercy and sent His Son (Rom. 3:21-5:21).

Remember our observation about John? Jesus came and met him and John shared openly about Jesus – but he didn't leave with Him and follow Him. That wasn't his call. He wasn't going on the far-flung adventure to distant places... he was to remain at home and do the work of pre-evangelism and early training of disciples...that was his call.

Don't you wonder if John wanted to quit the baptism gig and take off with his cousin Jesus to see the great things that would happen? Not everyone is called to that adventure. Some are called to quiet places of the deserts where parched men and women come in thirst and meet the messenger that has the words of life.

Observation 2: Some believers follow someone to Jesus, and then outgrow their first discipler, leaving on a great adventure of following Jesus personally (1:35-39).

For thousands of years, men were trained under an apprenticeship program. After their trainer felt they were ready, they joined a guild. When they gained all they could in the shop they were raised in, they were sent on the road and became "journeymen," learning their trade in guild shops in other villages. After a number of years, they returned home with a broader knowledge of the trade. They began a special work that would mark their ability – called their "masterpiece." When that piece was seen as worthy, they would begin training others, now called a "Maestro" or Master. The new Maestro was a reflection of his own master, but also a reflection of what he learned on the road as a journeyman.

John trained some men, including **Andrew** and **John** (implied) in John 1:35ff.

- Note that the men were disciples of JOHN before they became disciples of Jesus (1:35).
- It was John that pointed them to the Master of all (1:36).

- John had to be prepared to let them go to Jesus and follow on their own (1:37-38) – a painful step for a trainer.
- It was a credit to John's training that made them persistent in their following of Jesus and desire to grow in their personal knowledge of Him (1:39).

Note that the ends of the two followers – Andrew and John – play out differently: John became a pastor of Ephesus and a writer of a number of important NT letters. Andrew became an activist – reaching out to his brother Simon almost in the next breath after meeting and talking to Jesus.

The motor home has allowed us to put all the conveniences of home on wheels. A camper no longer needs to contend with sleeping in a sleeping bag, cooking over a fire, or hauling water from a stream. Now he can park a fully equipped home on a cement slab in the midst of a few pine trees and hook up to a water line, a sewer line and electricity. One motor home I saw recently had a satellite dish attached on top. No more bother with dirt, no more smoke from the fire, no more drudgery of walking to the stream. Now it is possible to go camping and never have to go outside. We buy a motor home with the hope of seeing new places, of getting out into the world. Yet we deck it out with the same furnishings as in our living room. Thus nothing really changes. We may drive to a new place, set ourselves in new surroundings, but the newness goes unnoticed, for we've only carried along our old setting.

The adventure of new life in Christ begins when the comfortable patterns of the old life are left behind.

Observation 3: Some confront a promise of God for them and it dramatically changes them, offering hope and utterly convincing them (1:40-42) – as in the case of Simon Peter.

Peter was initially led to Christ by his brother Andrew. Andrew brashly shared that Messiah had been found, and that was sufficient for the impulsive and boisterous Peter to follow (1:40-41). When Peter approached Jesus, the Savior offered a specific word of HOPE and PROMISE to Peter, and he was forever changed.

It is impossible to understand all that is involved in this, but I can say that what Peter heard marked a moment when he knew a decision had to be made...

Jonathon Falwell: Carrie Prejean, the California representative in this year's Miss USA competition in Las Vegas, was faced with one of these situations recently when she was asked before a national television audience to voice her perspective on same-sex marriage. In a now famous statement, Carrie replied, in part, "I do believe that marriage should be between a man and a woman; no offense to anybody out there. But that's how I was raised and I believe that it should be between a man and a woman."

As a result of this assertion which reflects her Christian faith, Carrie has been bitterly assailed by critics, most prominently by **homosexual activist and blogger Perez Hilton, who posed the question.** (It should be noted that **Carrie is a student at San Diego Christian College** so it is interesting, to say the least, that Mr. Hilton would target Carrie to answer the pointed query. But we know that God works in strange ways.)

On Wednesday, my brother Jerry Jr., the chancellor at Liberty University, introduced Carrie to our student body during a convocation service. She told students that the unexpected event has opened more doors than she ever dreamed possible to speak about her faith in Jesus Christ. "This has given me an opportunity to proclaim my faith with millions of people," she told a cheering Liberty University audience.

She said that when Mr. Hilton's question was posed, she immediately knew that she had come to a spiritual crossroads. "I knew right there that I was either going to please man or please God. And I knew there was no choice," she told our convocation audience. Then she reminded students that the Christian life is often full of challenges. "You're going to be persecuted, you're going to be made fun of and you're going to be called names. **But when you are given an opportunity to stand up for Christ, do it**," Carrie said with a radiant smile. "We deeply appreciate what you did," my brother (Jerry, Jr.) told her.

For each of the disciples of Jesus there is a moment of challenge and surrender of our hearts. For some it is dramatic, like Simon Peter - a few words, but a big change. For others, they surrender their hearts in quiet Sunday School rooms as small children. Nothing dramatic, humanly speaking, but something eternally powerful nonetheless…

Observation 4: Some believers are called by God even when they aren't looking for Him – chosen because He delights to do something specific in them for His glory (1:43-44) – as in the case of Philip!

John 1:43 simply says that Jesus came upon Philip of Bethsaida and told him to follow Him. Philip did it! He heard the word of Jesus, the tone of His voice, and looking into His eyes… he followed the Master.

We don't know what convinced Philip to follow. We know that he knew Andrew and Peter (and so did everyone else who lived in the village because they were loud mouths called "Sons of Thunder")! Whatever caused Philip to change his plans and begin to follow – it was compelling. I have met people who were called by Jesus in this way. They were living life without a thought of God, eternity, sin or anything of the sort. Yet, at a moment of God's choosing, He popped into their lives in an unmistakable way… and they could not resist the love of God.

Paul had his DAMASCUS ROAD SMACKDOWN by God when he was on a personal witch hunt against the cause of Christ.

You don't have to be looking for Jesus to find Him, but you do have to submit to Him to follow Him!

Observation 5: Some will not follow until they take their time and challenge everything they hear concerning Christ. Yet, when they truly meet Jesus, they are forever changed! (1:45-51).

Nathaniel wasn't quick to get on board. First, he had an issue with the origin of Jesus and His message – Nazareth wasn't a source that he could identify as valid at first (1:45-46). The testimony didn't make sense, and he wasn't just going to run after anyone that offered hope!

Jesus knows that most people don't really listen, but searching hearts are testing every word.

The story is told of Franklin Roosevelt who often endured long receiving lines at the White House. He complained that no one really paid any attention to what was said. One day, during a reception, he decided to try an experiment. To each person who came down the line and shook his hand, he murmured, "I murdered my grandmother this morning." The guests responded with phrases like, "Marvelous! Keep up the good work. We are proud of you. God bless you, sir." It was not till the end of the line, while greeting the ambassador from Bolivia, that his words were actually heard. Confused, the ambassador leaned over and whispered, "I'm sure she had it coming."

Nathaniel came to see Jesus, but questioned Him before he would get on board. (1:47-48). Jesus made claims and Nate questioned how Jesus could make them. Jesus didn't get upset – that isn't His way. He is not afraid to be tested, because He knows what is a real test from a seeking heart, and what is mockery and deceit.

When Jesus addressed him on a personal and heart level (something only the two of them truly grasped) Nathaniel was moved in his heart – and it came out his lips! (1:49).

Jesus offered Nathaniel even greater hope and promise for the adventure of giving Jesus his life to control! (1:50-51).

When we understand what God is doing in the people around us, we will see them as He sees them!

Knowing Jesus: Lessons in the Gospel of John (I)

Knowing Jesus
Lessons in the Gospel of John

Lesson Three: John 2:1-25 "The Surprising Savior"

Growing up in a small town in south Jersey, I had a lot of images and ideas about Who Jesus is. Was He the sullen, sunken eyed corpse that hung on the cross at the front of Paul VI Catholic Church a block behind my house? Was He the "flower power Jesus" of the Jesus Movement that was featured on the CBS special on "The New Church" when I was a kid. Was He the "Passover Plot" fake God that was shown in the movies when I was in High School? Was He the twisted religious teacher of "The DaVinci Code?"

Will the real Jesus please stand up?

John was written to clear up misunderstandings that were already taking place by the end of the first century. The Apostles were nearly all gone when John saw a plethora of "other works" rising in the church and confusion starting. By the close of the first century there were a number of interpretive methods already emerging from the young churches in the Mediterranean. There were in essence four important cities that emerged as the leading centers of Christianity, (along with lesser centers at Ephesus, Smyrna and Corinth):

> **Jerusalem:** A leader in the movement to call all believers into harmony with God's promises and restrictions to the Jewish people. There is ample evidence that they saw the new movement of believers as a reflection of promises and covenants God had made to the Jew in the "New Covenant" promises of Jeremiah 31. The best of this group simply wanted Gentiles to recognize God's special relationship with Israel, the worst of them wanted all Gentiles to become Jews to become followers of the New Covenant Way.

Alexandria: The home of allegorical belief. A number of early Christians came out of the Alexandrian community, and many reflected a view of the Bible that is frankly, hard to understand today. The most dangerous trends of Christian thought were derived from its works, many of which are now reflected in the *"Nag Hammadi Texts"* (Upper Egypt, found in 1945). The *Epistle of Barnabas*, an anti-Jewish and anti-literal diatribe with very strained spiritualized interpretation, illustrates this type of literature. The texts include the *Secret Gospels of Thomas and St. Mary Magdalene, Apocalypse of Peter*, and many others.

Antioch: Perhaps best illustrated later by the works of Ignatius, particularly those written as part of his journey to Rome (where he was thrown to the wild beasts by Emperor Trajan in about 110 CE). The works show a disdain for Jewish practices among believers, and is particularly short on quotes from the Hebrew Scriptures. The works are less extreme than Alexandrian literature, but included a light mix of allegory and a generally divorced view of the Jewish and Christian literatures.

Rome: Center of the "Christianities." The variety of thought is best illustrated in the diverse schools of Christian teaching. The *Apologist School* of Justin Martyr (110-165) reflects the notion that Jesus offered the revelation that began through men like Socrates and Plato. He had a particular bend against the Jewish claim to the Scriptures, and argued that Christians were the proper inheritors of the Word of God, as a Gentile born in the Samaritan city of Neapolis (modern Nablus). Opposing those notions were the reflections found in the *First Epistle of Clement of Rome* (fourth Bishop of Rome). His extensive knowledge and reference to the Hebrew Scriptures as principles made him a well-known Bible teacher.

Already by the end of the first century there were four distinct "Christianities" that were emerging, a thought that must have been troubling to John. Yet, confident in the power of the Word as he was, he knew the truth would change lives in a way that nothing else could.

How do you defend the Word? Like a roaring lion, you LET IT OUT and it will show its power to anyone who encounters it. If the church would but stick to the script, her power would return!

Key Principle: Jesus is not Who people think He is, and He breaks the molds we make for Him!

Nevertheless, John was paying attention to his flock in Ephesus when they needed guidance on Who Jesus is. He wrote the things He knew would help them understand Him.

He wrote of **seven life-changing works**:

- Water into wine (2:1-11): He can change ME!
- Long distance healing (4:46-54): He wants my TRUST!
- Lame man at Bethesda (5:1-11): He remembers when all forget.
- Loaves and fishes (6:6-13): His resources are inexhaustible.
- Storm on the Sea of Galilee (6:16-21): His strength is unlimited.
- The man born blind healed (9:1-7): He opens light to the darkness of man.
- The raising of Lazarus (11:1-45): He bring LIFE from death.

As we zero in on chapter two, there are **two stories** that cast Jesus in a light different than people normally think of Him.

The first story is that of the "**Wedding at Cana**" (John 2:1-13)

- On the third day there had been a wedding at Cana, and Jesus' mother was there (2:1).
- Jesus and His first five followers were invited (2:2) apparently arriving at the end of the feast.
- When the wine ran out, Mary called upon Jesus to address the problem (2:3), explaining they had run out of wine. She was evidently confident that Jesus was able to meet the need in some incredible way.
- Over Jesus' initial objections (2:4), she leaves Him with the servants, who are instructed to follow His commands (2:5).
- Jesus told the servants to take the six stone twenty to thirty gallon pots and fill them with water (a stunning violation of their purpose of ritual purity collection) (2:6-7).
- Jesus told them to draw out a cup from the stone jars and take it to the head cupbearer of the feast and have him sample it for the guests (2:8).
- The cupbearer was shocked and complimented the groom on his surprising stash of excellent wine (2:9-10)

What do we learn about Jesus from this important first miracle?

- We learn that Jesus wasn't so "other worldly" that He wouldn't celebrate a wedding with two people starting a new family.
- We observe that Jesus can make the ordinary into the extraordinary. God transforms the ordinary into the extraordinary, but only after the ordinary was set apart for His exclusive use. The water that was set aside for a specific use was put exclusively under the control of Jesus, and it was transformed into something greater.

God's intention for you is not that you become a **separatist** or a **conformist**. These extremes are safe, uneventful and apathetic...God wants you to follow in the footsteps of His Son, the timeless **transformist**. He is so passionate, so ridiculously fired up about it that He actually came in the flesh to model how it can and should be done. (CE Book)

Yet, there is something more surprising, more penetrating than either of those observations. Look again. Jesus got there and there was a problem. It was Mary his mother's problem, or at least she felt it was her problem. Watch in the text what she did. She identified a problem and then she thrust HER PLAN for the problem on Jesus.

Now I realize that Jesus was, at least from an earthly perspective, her son. Yet, think carefully about what the story can show us about the way believers act toward Jesus in their lives and their problems.

The text doesn't reveal that Mary dropped to her knees and sought God concerning the difficulty. In fact, she didn't even consult Jesus on what should be done. MARY HAD A LITTLE PLAN and she wanted her plan cared for by Jesus.

Did you ever do that? Did you ever decide that you knew what God SHOULD DO about something and then tell Him how it would honor Him?

Though Jesus was truthful to point out that she was pressing Him on issues out of their time, Jesus fulfilled the need. Why?

- Because she had a relationship with Jesus.
- Because she had a track record of faithfulness to Jesus.
- Because He chose to honor the request and not to embarrass her.

Yet, here should be a note of warning: We dare not tack Jesus on the plans we have. We are called to make Him our Master, not our Holy errand boy. We don't tell Him – He tells us! I recognize the problem of her being his mother makes this lesson more strained than many, but I trust that you recognize the tendency of a believer to fit God into his plans, and not wait on God to direct the plan. Why didn't she ask Him? Because she is like all of us who have a plan so good that even God should recognize it.

Think about it. Jesus may honor your request, and asks us to make requests to Him. Yet, the Word is not to be mistaken as an underhanded order from us to our Savior!

The second story is that of the "**First Cleansing of the Temple**" (John 2:13-25).

After Jesus performed His first miracle at the wedding in Cana, He traveled with His disciples and family to Capernaum ... about 15 miles away (2:12).

A few days later, Jesus journeyed south to Jerusalem for the **Passover** ... about 80 miles (as the crow flies) (2:13). Passover was so important we have some record of authorities that would repair the roads for the great influx of people ... and whitewash the tombs so nobody would accidentally touch them & defile themselves. Homes would be cleaned, cooking utensils washed, and the house was searched to make sure no leaven was found. Those living in Jerusalem were expected to put up guests, so they thoroughly cleaned their houses.

- Jews celebrated deliverance from bondage in Egypt and Jews from all over would come to the temple in Jerusalem to present their offerings.
- Animals would be slaughtered, fat would be burned, and blood would be sprinkled on the altar.
- Meat would be taken home, roasted, and eaten by the family. It was at this time that they would pay the temple tax of a silver ½ shekel coin.
- It was the biggest event of the year. Jesus went to the south porch of the temple where the main floor was covered with merchants selling animals and money-changers hawking the crowds as the best rate providers (2:14).

- The ½ shekel temple tax was being exchanged, and the place sounded more like a shuk or market than a place of worship and prayer. The sound of change and hawking drowned out the sound of the Levitical choir, and Jesus responded with open rebuke (2:15).
- The High Priest's family sold franchises for the concession stands to the various merchants and money-changers to the highest bidder. Merchants were charging inflated prices for sacrifice animals.
- Some reported that if you brought your own animal the priests would tell you that it was unclean and you had to purchase one of their "clean" animals. THEN - they would turn around and sell your "unclean" animal to someone else as a "clean" animal.
- NOTICE that Jesus didn't all of a sudden "lose it." He didn't fly off the handle. While He was walking around, observing the chaos, He probably picked up some of the leather cords that were laying around used to tie up the animals. While He was walking, He must have been tying them together into a small whip.

I sometimes wonder what God thinks of His "Church in the 21st Century." Have WE gotten off the path that He wanted us to follow? Have WE turned His house into a social club ... are we just going through the motions of worship? Have WE lost focus on true worship of our heavenly Father?

Someone has said: We worship our work. work at our play, and play at our worship.

God's plan is for His House to be a house of prayer, a special place, a place of worship and praise. *"My Father's house"* (2:16)

Jesus saw their attitude and actions. Jesus saw all the decorations of worship, but not the focus of worship!

We need to be **UNDISTRACTED** in our worship of God. Do we have Jesus' zeal of heart? (2:17) Do we say, *"I was glad when* *they said unto me, 'Let us go into the house of the Lord'"*? (cp. Psalm 69:9)

His zeal was eating Him up. He had a **PASSION** for the things of God.

We are passionate about our **sports**, our **eating**, **music**, our **work**. Are we that passionate about worship and prayer?

The authorities didn't ask about the nature of His dispute; that wasn't their issue. They wanted to know: "Who do You think You are to be doing this?" (2:18).

That was John's point – that very question. Who was Jesus anyway?

He was not willing for people to PLAY AT WORSHIP and mock a surrendered life before His Father!

Why didn't they stand up to Jesus? There were certainly more of them than Jesus and His few disciples. Because Jesus was operating with an authority that could be felt! They knew this was not simply some mad man....

What we see of Jesus' character in this passage is an accent to the **full picture of Who He is**. We are usually seeing His love and tenderness and mercy. God is love and certainly there is a majestic revelation of that here in John's gospel as well as in his epistles. But Christ's character and personality is perfectly balanced. It is a perfect blend of grace and truth. When the situation calls for **gentleness and tenderness He is kind**. But when the situation calls for **assertive leadership He does not shrink back** from the task.

I have watched the results of leadership that only defines godliness as a kind of passivity and maybe even complacency.

It's easier to just "let it go." But when something needs to be addressed, letting it go is not the answer.

The Chronicles of Narnia by C.S. Lewis was set in a world outside of our own. It's a world inhabited by centaurs, dwarves, talking wolves and beavers, fawns, and all kinds of mythical creatures. The **land of Narnia was covered in an endless winter** as the result of the cruel White Witch. And this world is just waiting for this winter to end. The central character of this book is a lion by the name of Aslan – and **Aslan represents Christ**.

And in *The Chronicles of Narnia* Lewis is asking what it would look like if Christ had to come to such a world to bring salvation. One of the differences between the book and the movie is the portrayal of Aslan. When the four children – Lucy, Edmund, Susan, and Peter – end up in Narnia Mr. and Mrs. Beaver tell them about Aslan. They learn that Aslan is the true King and the son of the "Emperor-Beyond-The-Sea." When they learn that Aslan is a lion – the Lion – and not a man, Susan says, "Is he – quite safe? I shall feel rather nervous about meeting a lion." Mr. Beaver replies, "If there's anyone who can appear before Aslan without their knees knocking, they're either braver than most or just quite silly." Then the youngest of the children, little Lucy, says, "Then he isn't safe?" To this question Mr. Beaver replies, "Who said anything about safe? 'Course he's not safe. But he's good."

Jesus is not Who people think He is, and He breaks the molds we make for Him!

Knowing Jesus
Lessons in the Gospel of John

Lesson Four: John 3:1-21 "The Total Makeover"

A number of popular TV series were obsessed with taking houses and even people to "remake" them. Each reworked the externals of their project. Jesus claimed that no one can reform, conform, or be informed into the Kingdom - (externally oriented change) - it was entered only by complete miraculous inner transformation!

The story of Nicodemus is set up by the penetrating truth offered at the end of John 2.

*John 2:24 But Jesus, on His part, was not entrusting Himself to them, for He knew all men, 25 and because He did not need anyone to testify concerning man, for **He Himself knew what was in man**.*

The story in the beginning of John 3 is an illustration of **how Jesus could read the heart of a man**, albeit a man of stature and importance.

John 3:1 is short, but PACKED with information to set up Jesus' ability to see through the outer layer of Nicodemus.

*John 3:1 Now there was a man of the Pharisees, named **Nocodemus**, a ruler of the Jews.*

The "man of the Pharisees" was seen by others as a man of **POSITION** and **PIETY**. You couldn't have raised a more moral son than Nicodemus. If anyone "deserved" eternal life, it would appear that Nicodemus had all the right qualifications. He seems worthy of eternal life.

But the scripture reminds us that salvation is not about human effort or merit. Nicodemus held a distinguished religious position.

- *Position does not save you.*
- *Being a pastor doesn't save you.*
- *Being a Sunday school teacher doesn't save you.*
- *Being a choir director doesn't save you.*
- *Being a member of a church doesn't save you.*
- *Being a good mom or dad doesn't save you.*
- *Being born again is not about positions.*

The man "named Nicodemus" was named in Greek "conqueror of the people" or "the people's champion" (victor). The name suggests **POPULARITY**. *Popularity does not save you.* Being born again is not about popularity. A Hebrew form of the name (Naqdimon) is found in the Talmud, often shortened to Naqai – so, if you add verse two, he is the original "Nick at night." ☺ Surely it was given to a man with a great family – that suggests a great **PEDIGREE**.

3:2 This man came to Jesus by night and said to Him, "Rabbi, we know that You have come from God as a teacher; for no one can do these signs that You do unless God is with him."

The next phrase in verse one is "ruler of the Jews," a statement of obvious **POWER** and **PRESTIGE** in the community. *Power and prestige does not save you.* Nicodemus possessed both. He was a man of dignity & a man of righteousness. He lived his life studying scripture & doing the right things. He spent his life fasting & praying, studying the law & studying the scripture. He was religious – but he was lost. Being born again is not about prestige & piety.

You see, being born again is not about human efforts – it's about a **personal relationship** which is from above. New birth is not something we do, it's **something God does through the power of the Holy Spirit** - and it's a miraculous thing. Being born again is an **intervention** from God that leads to a

TRANSFORMATION by God. This supernatural act of God takes the Holy Spirit & implants the Spirit into our hearts – He gives us a heart transplant. It causes us to be a changed creature.

Key Principle: You cannot INFORM your way to Heaven, REFORM your way in, CONFORM your way in – you must allow God to TRANSFORM you.

Nicodemus was all about the externals, and that was his primary problem. He was all about RELIGION. Religion is all about standards and conformity – man's desperate attempt to please God by DOING SOMETHING that will win the Creator's love and forgiveness.

Even today, religious groups are known by external characteristics:

How many Christians does it take to change a light bulb?

> **Pentecostal**: Ten – One to change the bulb & nine to pray against the spirit of darkness
> **Presbyterians**: None – The lights will go off & on at predestined times
> **Roman Catholics**: None – Candles only
> **Baptists**: At least 15 – One to change the bulb and three committees to approve the change & decide who brings the potato salad & fried chicken
> **Episcopalians**: Three – One to call the electrician, one to mix the drinks and one to talk about how much better the old one was.
> **Methodists**: Undetermined – Whether your light is bright, dull, or completely out, you are loved. You can be a light bulb, turnip bulb, or tulip bulb. Church wide lighting service is planned for Sunday. Bring bulb of your choice and a covered dish.
> **Lutherans**: None – Lutherans don't believe in change.

Amish: What's a light bulb? (original author unknown)

Nicodemus has **three statements** that were captured in the Gospel account. If you look closely at them, they reflect three assumptions that still plague people and keep them from understanding salvation by *grace*:

Statement 1: John 3:2 This man came to Jesus by night and said to Him, "Rabbi, we know that You have come from God as a teacher; for no one can do these signs that You do unless God is with him."

Look closely at what Nicodemus was saying.

First, his words were essentially incorrect. It was NOT TRUE that only God's presence could bring about miraculous events. If he looked carefully at Exodus 4:3, he would see that God could make a staff into a serpent that would scare even Moses! Later, in the hands of Aaron his brother, they stood before Pharaoh in Exodus 7. The eighty year old Moses and eighty-three year old Aaron saw God perform this same miracle in Pharaoh's court. Yet, Pharaoh's black magic men were able to do the same. Unfortunately for them, Aaron's serpent ate all of theirs – leaving them "staff-less" in the end! The sad account should remind us that JUST BECAUSE A MIRACLE TAKES PLACE, DOES NOT MEAN GOD INITIATED IT. Nor does it imply He is on board with the deliverer! Nick, your opening statement is just plain false.

Second, in addition to being wrong, Nick's opening line gave away the wrong assumption of his heart. **Nicodemus assumed that the externals were accurate proof of internals**. Another way of saying it, perhaps more clearly, is: **YOU CAN SEE ON THE OUTSIDE WHAT SOMEONE IS ON THE INSIDE**.

This is wrong on every level, but it is the normal stuff of religious people. They believe that what you see is what is there, because they focus on the external life as an indicator of the inner life. The problem is **I CAN CONFORM TO LOOKING LIKE A BELIEVER!** Jesus took apart the assumption in His answer…

Answer 1: John 3:3 Jesus answered and said to him, "Truly, truly, I say to you, unless one is born again he cannot see the kingdom of God."

Jesus offered a complete counter to the idea that externals offer accurate proof of internal conditions of a man. He says essentially two things:

First, it is possible to see the kingdom of God – but there is an unshakeable requirement. He offers only one method to this end, with no exception.

Second, Jesus offered the words that set Nicodemus back on his heels. Jesus said that one can see the kingdom ONLY if they are REBORN. Jesus reversed the external proof to a TOTAL TRANSFORMATION that comes from inside out.

Because of my Jewish education, I do feel compelled to mention that *The Talmud* uses the term "born again" of **proselytes who underwent the conversion ritual** for a Gentile that wanted to join the covenant of Israel. An immersion into water as part of the process was termed a "re-creation" as an Israelite. Under rabbinic law, Gentiles reborn as Jews were "new creatures" whose prior family relationships were no longer binding. Everything in his or her life became new. Nicodemus would, no doubt, have been familiar with this ceremony and the words surrounding it. One way to read his question concerning this statement is "How can a Jew re-become a Jew?" It is hard to say how much this played into the conversation.

What is clear is that **birth is a perfect analogy of an "inside to outside" transformation**. Men struggle to have any attachment to a "not yet born" child. I wrote a series of letters to Rachel, our first born, prior to her birth. I watched with amazement as the lump moved on my wife's belly. I smiled as we both felt little kicks from her hidden legs. Yet, in all of it, she seemed like a lump to me. She wasn't yet a cooing and smiling baby. She was a moving lump inside a belly, and it is hard to get attached to that! It was in the delivery room I saw that lump transformed into a living, breathing baby girl! What an amazing event!

The point of the statement that "only by being born again" is this: *Nicodemus, you must totally rethink your premise. Entering the Kingdom is NOT by conforming to a set of rules or reforming your lifestyle to a certain set of rules.* **It is being transformed by a process YOU DO NOT CONTROL!** That seemed remarkable, and Nicodemus offered several questions.

Statement 2: John 3:4 Nicodemus said to Him, "How can a man be born when he is old? He cannot enter a second time into his mother's womb and be born, can he?"

Nicodemus shows another big assumption of his life. The first assumption we saw above was **YOU CAN SEE ON THE OUTSIDE WHAT SOMEONE IS ON THE INSIDE**. We saw that was a **FALSE** assumption.

Look at what he asked Jesus. First he wanted to know if Jesus was saying that an old man could be physically born. In his second question he gets even more graphic and questions the possibility of entering the womb anew. How ridiculous! Maybe, but again he tips his hand and shows the misunderstanding of his heart.

His second assumption is as false as his first one. He is in effect thinking: **SPIRITUAL CHANGE OCCURS BECAUSE OF PHYSICAL CHANGES YOU MAKE**. Another way of saying this is **MY INSIDE CHANGES BY STUFF I DO OUTSIDE**. If I am to be "born again" it must be a physical thing – and that doesn't make sense.

This is the call of the works based salvation of a great many religious faiths. Do these works, wear these clothes, use these terms... then you will be saved. The problem is that is all **OUTSIDE CHANGE** and (as Jesus showed already above) the outside is an unreliable indicator of the inside heart condition.

Nicodemus assumed that Jesus was speaking physically, and that He wasn't making any sense. Truthfully, it didn't make sense because the answer went beyond the places Nicodemus normally sought for answers – into the God-controlled spirit realm. That is a terribly uncomfortable place for a worker that thinks he is earning his way into the Kingdom.

Maybe this will help you grasp the problem: Three men died and were standing at the pearly gates. What have you done to deserve Heaven? 1st—police officer, enforced law, fought crime. Peter, "OK, go on in." 2nd—very wealthy and gave lots of money to charitable causes. Peter, "OK, go on in." 3rd—director of an HMO organization, helped save millions of dollars for health care and insurance companies, helped cut down on waste, fraud, and abuse in the system. Peter, "OK come on in, but you can only stay for 3 days.

We have all heard jokes about people showing up at the pearly gates seeking entrance into Heaven. While many of these jokes bring a smile to our faces, behind most of them is **the false assumption that we must do something to get into Heaven**. It is shocking to people to hear that they can't do anything to earn entrance into Heaven.

Grace marches beyond human comprehension. By nature, we want to earn and then deserve God's favor. Grace scandalously challenges our natural way of thinking.

    Answer 2: Jesus countered his questions with a series of important and careful statements.

John 3:5 Jesus answered, "Truly, truly, I say to you, unless one is born of water and the Spirit he cannot enter into the kingdom of God. 6 That which is born of the flesh is flesh, and that which is born of the Spirit is spirit. 7 Do not be amazed that I said to you, 'You must be born again.' 8 The wind blows where it wishes and you hear the sound of it, but do not know where it comes from and where it is going; so is everyone who is born of the Spirit."

Look at the **three points** of His response:

First, two types of birth are necessary to be in the kingdom – a physical birth and a spiritual birth.
Second, the two are distinct from one another – but both are transformational events.
Third, those born of the spirit are compared to the wind – the **effects** of wind can be seen without the **work** of the wind being displayed. In the same way, the effect of the spirit's transformation can be observed, but not the work – for it is NOT PHYSICAL.

It is the nature of religious people to look for ways to observe God's hand – even when He doesn't choose to display it. Ironically, the church movements that began with an emphasis on the work of the Spirit have found themselves tilting quickly into a theology that emphasizes blessing in the physical world... even though Jesus seems to say they are not reliably connected – at least in appearance. Can the Spirit be doing a great transforming work inside someone and people around them are unable to tell? Yes, for a while. But like the wind, things will get moved around in their life and it will eventually show!

Statement 3: *John 3:9 Nicodemus said to Him, "How can these things be?"*

In itself it seems impossible to know if Nicodemus was replying with an honest question. It is true that he eventually became a follower of Jesus, and that he was a part of the burial of Jesus along with Joseph of Arimathea. He eventually got there. Yet, the more I read Jesus' answer to this encounter with Nicodemus, the more **I am convinced that Nicodemus wasn't buying the spiritual formula of transformation**. His assumption was, **IF IT DOESN'T FIT MY PHYSICAL SENSE OF UNDERSTANDING, IT MUST BE NONSENSE**! Jesus poured it on at the end with a rather detailed reply to his question. Parts of it seemed pretty **abrupt** and **hard**.

Answer 3: *John 3:10 Jesus answered and said to him, "Are you the teacher of Israel and do not understand these things? 11 Truly, truly, I say to you, we speak of what we know and testify of what we have seen, and you do not accept our testimony. 12 If I told you earthly things and you do not believe, how will you believe if I tell you heavenly things? 13 No one has ascended into Heaven, but He who descended from Heaven: the Son of Man. 14 As Moses lifted up the serpent in the wilderness, even so must the Son of Man be lifted up 15 so that whoever believes will in Him have eternal life. 16 For God so loved the world that He gave His only begotten Son, that whoever believes in Him shall not perish, but have eternal life. 17 For God did not send the Son into the world to judge the world, but that the world might be saved through Him. 18 He who believes in Him is not judged; he who does not believe has been judged already, because he has not believed in the name of the only begotten Son of God. 19 This is the judgment, that the Light has come into the world, and men loved the darkness rather than the Light, for their deeds were evil. 20 For everyone who does evil hates the Light, and does not come to the Light for fear that his deeds will be exposed. 21 But he who practices the truth comes to the Light, so that his deeds may be manifested as having been wrought in God."*

The answer Jesus gives is detailed, but absolutely essential to understand:

First, a teacher of God's people should understand transformation by the Spirit (it is required!).

Second, this is not a theory, and not an option (3:11).

Jesus was pointed – you haven't been accepting our testimony! Jesus HAS THE POWER to judge, and we must never forget that!

When John F. Kennedy was President of the United States, Life magazine published photos of his children, John Jr. and Caroline, playing with their toys on the floor of the Oval Office. Those images captured the hearts of the American people like nothing before or since. Why? I think it's because it bridged a gap between two thoughts: Kennedy was the President of the United States, but he was also a father. He held ultimate political power in the Free World, but playing at his feet were two little kids who called him Daddy. Why? He was their father. He was not only President of the United States, he was also their dad. In the same way, God is both our Father and the Lord of glory. We can approach Him confidently in prayer because we are His dearly beloved children, but, we must never forget that He is also the Sovereign of the universe. (David Jeremiah, *Prayer, the Great Adventure*, pp. 89-90)

Third, failure to grab the transformation will block other truth from the heart (3:12).

Fourth, the truth of transformation has only one source – Me! (3:13).

Fifth, failure to get behind this message will block the ability to lead others to eternal life (3:14-15).

In Numbers 21 after the nation of Israel had experienced a military victory against King Arad the Canaanite, they began to embark on a journey that brought much discouragement (v. 4). With this discouragement they began to speak against God and against Moses (v. 5). This prompted God to send fiery serpents among the people. The people who were bitten began to die (v. 6). After this the people went to Moses admitting their sin, and requesting that Moses pray to God for their deliverance. The Lord told Moses in verse 8 of Numbers 21, *"Make a fiery serpent, and set it on a standard; and it shall come about, that everyone who is bitten, when he looks at it, he will live."* Moses did that and the people lived when they looked to the brazen serpent.

Sixth, My coming is to SAVE, not judge (3:16-17). I don't bring God's wrath (a message many others have given before Me) but I bring God's **MERCY AND GRACE**.

Let's imagine that you are driving and through carelessness you jump a curb, damage your car and knock down and destroy a city sign. Now, the police officer arrives on the scene. He surveys the scene and you admit that the accident was your fault so he gives you a ticket for careless driving. The officer assigns you a court date and informs you that the city will be in touch so that you can pay for a new sign - that's justice - deserved punishment. But let's say out of the goodness of his heart the officer says, "Well, I know this can happen to anybody and you've already got to pay for the damage to your car so I'll just let it go, no ticket and you don't have to pay for the sign." You'd say, "That's incredible," but that's **MERCY** - exemption from punishment. But let's say that the officer is really generous and he tells you, you're not going to get a ticket; but not only that-but he pulls out his check book and writes you a check to pay for the full amount of the damage done to your car and further, he tells you that "He'll pay the city for the damaged sign and your ticket too." You say, "That's impossible!" But that's

GRACE. Favor given when punishment is deserved. (Adapted from illustration Timothy Smith contributed to Sermon Central)

Seventh, the **sole basis** of judgment is belief in My Word. People choose not to believe, because they prefer to live under the darkness of their own controls! (3:18-21).

Someone asked George Whitfield, "Why do you always preach, "You must be born again?" He replied, "Because you must be born again!"

God wants us to seriously listen to His heart!

Isa.1:18 says, "Come now, and let us reason together," says the LORD, "Though your sins are like scarlet, they shall be as white as snow; though they are red like crimson, they shall be as wool."

How? By something I DO? By REFORMATION? NO!

God says:

Rom.3:10 says, There is none righteous, no, not one.

Rom.3:23 For all have sinned and fall short of the glory of God.

Rom.6:23 For the wages of sin is death, but the gift of God is eternal life in Christ Jesus our Lord. This teaches us that we cannot earn salvation, that our sin earns us eternal death, and that Jesus gives us eternal life.
Rom.10:9 If you confess with your mouth the Lord Jesus and believe in your heart that God has raised Him from the dead, you will be saved.
Rom.10:13 says, For whoever calls on the name of the LORD shall be saved
Psa.103:12 says, As far as the east is from the west, So far has He removed our transgressions from us.

You cannot INFORM your way to Heaven, REFORM your way in, CONFORM your way in – you must allow God to TRANSFORM you.

Knowing Jesus
Lessons in the Gospel of John

Lesson Five: John 3:22-36 "Father Loves Most"

A quick look at the important "dads "of America shows quite a variety of ideas about what a father should be:

- Jim Anderson — Father Knows Best
- Ward Cleaver — Leave it to Beaver
- Sheriff Andy Taylor — The Andy Griffith Show
- Howard Cunningham — Happy Days
- Mike Brady -- The Brady Bunch
- Charles Ingalls -- Little House on the Prairie
- Tim "The Tool Man" Taylor — Home Improvement
- Archie Bunker -- All in the Family
- Steve Keaton -- Family Ties
- Al Bundy -- Married with Children (not even a reference to his role as father…)
- Cliff Huxtable -- The Cosby Show"
- Homer Simpson -- The Simpsons
- Danny Tanner — Full House

Why is it that when we say the word "father" to a group, the ideas that are most often voiced are not positive? Could the role models we have seen be confusing to us?

The radio show begun in 1949, with Robert Young as father, was called "Father Knows Best." The TV show that followed in the 1950's mirrored a rosy picture of American society in the 1950's suburbs, and ran until Young left in 1960. The show highlighted a father's wisdom, wit, and loving nature.

Tucked into the Gospel of John is **another story of a loving Father**. This picture is found in an obscure, **tiny sermon** of John the Baptizer, the cousin of Jesus, given to his followers before

Jesus really got His popular ministry in "high gear." In the sermon, John shared a pattern of godliness that sustained him through the end of his ministry. In addition, he shared a startling truth that made it possible for John to submit his life's work to Jesus!

Key Principle: Because of the Father's love for His Son, He offered authority and supreme trust. A real follower of Jesus can offer no less!

The central story of the Bible is rooted in the LOVE of God the Father. In the beginning there was a family unity – a loving Father, a cherished Son, and an intimate and loving Spirit.

Why is it so hard for many today to picture our Father in Heaven as **driven by LOVE**? There are perhaps **three reasons**:

- Many people are growing up in homes without a father, and have no emotional connection to their biological father.
- Some are growing up in homes with fathers that are both immature emotionally and unhelpful in their growth as children. When these children grow, they have a distorted view of a father's role – because of the sin of their father.
- A media culture has deliberately trashed the image of a father. Writer and producers, some who were likely hurt by their own fathers, have used the airwaves to project this as the message of the norm, quietly faulting the natural world for introducing such clumsy and brutish figures into the world.

Now *Lifetime TV*, a network known for its movies about women being endangered by men, offers a "so called reality" program called "**Deadbeat Dads**." In the beginning of gotcha TV, viewers enjoyed watching the police bust down a door and haul away the bad guy on a show like "**Cops**." That same format migrated over **to Animal Planet**, where the cops bust down the door and arrest the man who has been starving his dogs or kicking his cats. Now Lifetime is doing the same thing to **divorced fathers**.

The *Lifetime TV* program **ignores the numbers**. More than **90 percent** of fathers with joint custody paid the support due, according to a Census Bureau report (Series P-23, No. 173). So **deadbeats are in the minority**. Also, most so-called deadbeat dads actually are dead broke. Two-thirds of men who fail to make child-support payments earn poverty-level wages, according to the Federal Office of Child Support Enforcement. Most of the others are unemployed. Bruce Walker, executive coordinator at the District Attorneys Council in Oklahoma City, who ran the state's child-support enforcement program for three years and jailed hundreds of fathers for nonpayment, told the *Newark Star-Ledger* in 2002: "These men are seldom the mythical monsters described by politicians. Many times I prosecuted impoverished men," he told the *Star-Ledger*. "I prosecuted one deadbeat dad who had been hospitalized for malnutrition and another who lived in the bed of a pickup truck." Nor is it likely that Lifetime will ever show that some fathers simply give money directly to their teenage children because some mothers end up using child-support payments for everything but the child. Child visitation and child support are tied together, at least in the minds of many fathers. The largest federally funded study of child-support payments was led by Arizona State University researcher Sanford Braver over an eight-year period. Mr. Braver found that fathers with joint custody pay 90.2 percent of all child support ordered. Fathers with visitation rights pay 79.1 percent of all child support ordered. However, fathers with no access or visitation rights to their children pay just 44.5 percent of the court-ordered child support. Much of Mr. Braver's data was backed up in the Census Bureau report. (Series P-23, No. 173)

Without a view of manly but loving behavior, we have a crisis of sexually confused and immature young men growing in this generation.

Actually, in our society, you wouldn't think men played much of a role at all in the family. But that is NOT how the Bible views parents.

Proverbs 6:20 Listen, my son, to your father's instruction and do not forsake your mother's teaching. They will be a garland to grace your head and a chain to adorn your neck.

Proverbs 1:8-9 Again, Solomon tells his son: *My son, keep your father's commands and do not forsake your mother's teaching.*

I want to take a few minutes and look at a godly man with godly attitudes as he attempted to correct his followers in their ungodly attitudes. Our story from John 3 may seem an unlikely place to talk about fathers, but it is actually quite a natural place. The record is primarily a mini-message of John the Baptizer to his followers.

To understand the message of John, the writer includes **three important details** about the setting:

- Jesus and His disciples were baptizing at another location at the same time as John, His cousin, continued the baptism work at Aenon near Salim. The crowds to Jesus' ministry appeared to be increasing, while John's work was shrinking and giving way to the new work (3:22-24).
- John's disciples were feeling on the defensive because they were being questioned by an unidentified man in the crowd about their practices (3:25).
- John's disciples apparently felt a disappointment over the shrinking crowds. Remember, they lost some of their own fellow disciples to Jesus (see John 1:37ff).

John's mini-sermon is recorded in John 3:27-36. The sermon revealed **seven critical character traits** that John wanted his disciples to understand about a man and his relationship with God.

Seven Character Traits of a Godly Man:

> **CONFIDENCE:** (3:27) John soothed the envious hearts of his disciples with these words – "You get what God gives you!" Out of context these words could be used for one who was simply hiding laziness, but that isn't what was going on here! John was acknowledging the reality of a sovereign God, and the need to be content in His hands. Godly men and women lose their self-confidence and gain a God-confidence!

John was courageously confident about what God had in store for him. **That kind of confidence is like going after Moby Dick with a rowboat, a harpoon and a jar of tartar sauce.**

Imagine that you are an ice skater in competition. You are in first place with one more round to go. If you perform well, the trophy is yours. You're nervous, anxious, and frightened. Then, only minutes before your performance, your trainer rushes over to you with the thrilling news: "You've already won!" The judges tabulated the scores and the person in second place can't catch you. You are too far ahead. Upon hearing that news, how will you feel? Exhilarated? And how will you skate? --- Timidly? Cautiously? Of course not! How about courageously and confidently? You bet you will. You will do your best because the prize is yours. You will skate like a champion because that is what you are!

> **POSITION:** (3:28) John knew the purpose and place of his life was not to be the center of anyone's universe. Only a mature godly man understands this. We all have a deep longing to be the center of someone's universe – but our place as believers is help others put their relationship with the Lord at the center – not the relationship with US. John knew he was a POINTER not a CENTER. Godly men and

women answer the question, "Father, what have You made me to be?"

JOY: (3:29) John wasn't simply sure that he wasn't the center of the world – he learned the secret of taking JOY in being what God created him to be. He didn't "settle" for his lot in life, he REVELED in the joy that came with an understanding that his very value in life came from his joyful dwelling in his identity as the close friend of the groom. Godly men and women seek to take the joy of the journey on each step with them – the resolute assurance that God has not lost interest in them, nor lost the ability to care for them.

MICHAEL CARD tells the story of a man named Joseph who came to Christ out of a Muslim background. One day walking a hot dirty African road met someone who shared Christ with him. Then and there he accepted Jesus as his Savior and the power of the Holy Spirit overwhelmed him with such joy that the first thing he wanted to do was go back and tell his own village. He went from door to door telling of the cross and the forgiveness for sin. He expected their faces to light up as his had when they discovered this wonderful truth. To his amazement they became violent: the men seized him and held him to the ground while the women beat him with strands of barbed wire. Dragged and left to die alone in the bush. He revived and made it to a water hole where he spent days recovering. He was confused and finally decided that he must have left something out or not told the story correctly. After rehearsing the message he returned, stood in the circle of huts, and began to proclaim Jesus. Again he was grabbed by men and beaten by women, reopening the wounds that had just begun to heal. He was dragged unconscious again and left to die. To have survived the first time was remarkable but to survive this beating was a miracle. Days later he awoke and determined to go back. This time he was attacked before he even opened his mouth. Before he passed out the last thing he saw was that the women who were beating him had begun to weep. This time he awoke in his own bed, the ones who had beaten him were now trying to save his life. The entire village came to know Jesus Christ.

> **CLARITY:** (3:30) One cannot read the words: "He must increase and I must decrease!" and not recognize the crystal clear sound of a voice that has embraced TRUTH. John knew he wasn't the main character in the drama being played out. Godly men and women always know this. If the story is about US, then it is not about God's Son!

A person who calls himself frank and candid can very easily find Proverbs 6:20 becoming tactless and cruel. A person who prides himself on being tactful can find eventually that he has become evasive and deceitful. A person with firm convictions can become pigheaded. A person who is inclined to be temperate and judicious can sometimes turn into someone with weak convictions and banked fires of resolution . . . Loyalty can lead to fanaticism. Caution can become timidity. Freedom can become license. Confidence can become arrogance. Humility can become servility. All these are ways in which strength can become weakness. (Dore Schary, *Bits & Pieces,* December 9, 1993, pp. 3-4)

It is only by connecting our lives to the truth – seeing clearly what God says, that we can take our weaknesses and allow them to become our strength!

> **SUBMISSION:** (3:31) John answered his disciples' complaints with a straightforward claim that Jesus is Lord from Heaven, and worthy of all submission. No man or woman can ever truly be considered godly who does not understand full and complete submission. It doesn't mean we will live every moment with our spiritual knees bowed, but it means that is the GOAL.
>
> **DISCERNMENT:** (3:32-34) John claimed that Jesus spoke that which He knew first hand, that it was the very truth of the Words of God and that it was infused with the limitless

power of the Spirit of God. He trusted what Jesus taught, and he had the discernment to see it as truth and label it as such. Godliness presupposes the ability to discern truth from nonsense. No godly man or woman will truly walk as they ought without discernment that acts as a screen to filter out the false and allow the truth to permeate.

George Hunter contends that the first characteristic of a secular person in the modern world is that he or she is ignorant of basic Christianity. It has been said of the Baby Boomers, those born between 1963 and 1977 and the first generation to grow up in a postmodern context, that they lack even the memory of a hope-giving gospel. Today many people outside of the church struggle with the concept of Christ's deity. They think he was a good man, perhaps even a prophet, but not God in human form. Further, 72 percent of Americans now deny the existence of absolute truth, and few have confidence in the historical accuracy or ethical authority of the Bible. Two-thirds of the population does not know what John 3:16 refers to, and less than four out of every ten Americans have any idea what the term gospel means. Ten percent believe that the name of Noah's wife was Joan of Arc. (James White, Rethinking the Church, p. 41)

> **UNDERSTANDING:** (3:35-36) John shared the DEPTH of understanding of the larger picture of the world. He was not so ego bound that all he could perceive was how everything affected him – he was a man with a bigger picture in front of him. It is within this larger frame that everything God was calling him to do made real sense. John understood that God was from the beginning a God of relationship. He loved, and because of that, it was easy for God the Father to offer authority to the Son. If the Father could do that, so could John! He loved Jesus, so surrendering crowds and accolades to Him was not a sacrifice he couldn't accept!

That understanding is where the great truth was revealed from John's lips. Because John saw that the Father in Heaven loved the Son, and trusted the Son completely - John could follow suit and give up any position, title, fame or importance to Jesus. God - out of love - gave the Son authority. How could John give less than his passing fame?

In the end, every believer must surrender his life's fortune, fame, power, and pleasure to the One he serves. John saw the pattern from the Father and responded in love.

Shouldn't we surrender in love as well?

Because of the Father's love for His Son, He offered authority and supreme trust. A real follower of Jesus can offer no less! We have the salvation and love of God, because the **Father loved MOST.**

Knowing Jesus
Lessons in the Gospel of John

Lesson Six: John 4:1-54 "I Object!"

We have all seen it. The lawyer jumps to his feet in the midst of his opponent taking apart the logic of the witness on the stand. "I object!" the lawyer shouts. The line of the questions is broken, and the rhythm of the opponent is slowed. It is a strategic move, and sometimes a tactic.

Key Principle: We often place road blocks in the direction Jesus offers, but He knows how to deal with our objections.

The story is a simple and familiar dialogue between Jesus and the woman at the Sychar well. It is easy to divide the story into **three parts**, as John recalls the events:

- The Setting (4:1-6)
- The Exchange (4:7-28)
- The Results (4:29-42) (next lesson)

Because John says that he is deliberately attempting to show character and power traits in Jesus to allow one to believe and have life (John 20:30-31), the story's primary purpose is to reveal the truth about Jesus. Along the way, we meet the unnamed woman, her fellow Samaritan villagers, and the disciples.

The Setting: (4:1-6)

Jesus became aware that the Pharisees were "bean counting," trying to measure the rise in popularity of Jesus over John, and He made a hasty retreat from them. He had no desire to get caught up in the certain celebrity status that He would soon be afforded, so He left. He arrived close to midday and asked His disciples to go into town and get something for them to eat. Though normal water gathering was made in the early morning and late afternoon, a woman appeared to draw water at an unusual hour – as Jesus was propped beside the well.

Jesus and the woman had a verbal exchange that has become familiar to many Bible students. The discussion helps us see the kinds of objections that are common when people are confronted with the truth of Jesus; and how Jesus was able to answer the objections with direct and important claims.

There is a contrast between Nicodemus (chapter 3) and the Samaritan woman (cha**pter 4):**

• **Nicodemus is an example** of the truth that no one can rise so high as to be ABOVE the need for salvation.

• The **Samaritan woman is an example** of the truth that no one can sink so low as to be BELOW the offer of salvation.

The Exchange: Objections People Raise to Jesus and His Message: (4:7-28)

Doubt of Intention: What does Jesus really want from me? (4:9). Clearly the woman was stunned that Jesus as a Jew would ask her as a Samaritan for something to drink. Yet, on more careful examination, it appears that she was not only asking why a Jew would speak to her, but she was exposing a very basic reaction that many people have when Jesus reaches out to them.

The Gospel *offers* something to each person, but it also *requires* something of them. **It requires that an individual trust Jesus, and obey what He asks of them. Without submission of the will there is no real salvation.** Jesus began ASKING FOR HER TO DO SOMETHING FOR HIM. The simple act of giving a drink to Jesus was an act of obedience – an act of trust. She was a woman alone, and this man may have had MANY ideas on his mind. She didn't know Him, and her history was such that we would not be surprised to find out that she didn't trust Him right away.

> **Sense of Unworthiness**: **How can you deal with someone LIKE ME?** The misconception that people carry in their minds about Jesus is that He spent His time with religious people in clean and tidy places. That is not the Jesus of the Gospels. At the same time, a Samaritan woman aptly pointed to a true breach in the relationship between Jews and Samaritans that did exist. Prejudices existed on both sides, and clearly this woman has encountered them, or simply possessed them. Whether she felt an intense unworthiness as a Samaritan is not the whole issue. It is clear that she felt that Jesus would perceive her as inferior.

That is the key: people are confronted by Jesus and they react because they know themselves. Little do they realize that this is a form of a worshipful reaction (cp. Isaiah 6) to see one's own sinfulness in the light of God's truth and perfection!

Jesus' answer was direct to her – **You are worried about who you are and what I may really want**. That is the **wrong focus**. If you refocus on **Who I am**, you will find a gift is awaiting you! (4:10). In order for her to receive the gift, she needed to **THIRST TO KNOW HIM**!

Have you ever been thirsty? I don't mean the average thirst where a drink of water sounds good after a long walk or after working in the garden on a hot summer day. I mean really -- really thirsty…where your tongue sticks to the roof of your mouth and you have to peel your lips off of your teeth and all you can think about is water.

In 1996, a young marine corporal named Joey Mora was standing on a platform of an aircraft carrier patrolling the Iranian Sea. Incredibly, he fell overboard. His absence was not known for 36 hours. A search and rescue mission began, but was given up after another 24 hours. No one could survive in the sea without even a lifejacket after 60 hours. His parents were notified that he was "missing and presumed dead."

The rest of the story is one of those "truth is stranger than fiction" events. Scriptwriters would pass it up as "not believable." Four Pakistani fishermen found Joey Mora about 72 hours after he had fallen from the aircraft carrier. He was treading water in his sleep, clinging to a makeshift floatation device made from his trousers -- a skill learned in most military survival training. He was delirious when they pulled him into their fishing boat. His tongue was dry and cracked and his throat parched.

Just about two years later, as he spoke with Stone Philips of NBC Dateline, he recounted an unbelievable story of will to live and survival. Who would not give up? He said it was God Who kept him struggling to survive. His discovery by the fishermen makes searching for a needle in a haystack a piece of cake. The most excruciating thing of all? Joey said that the one thought that took over his body and pounded in his brain was "Water!" (*NBC Date Line*: Nov. 1998)

> **Doubt of His Ability**: Jesus made an overt claim that He had something to GIVE the woman, but she couldn't see how it was possible for Jesus to deliver on the promises (4:11). She chided, "You don't think you are greater than our fathers, do you? (4:12). Wrapped in her question is one of the oldest forms of objection to Jesus and His message. She wanted to compare Jesus to other great men, and didn't see how He could claim to offer more than other men of seemingly greater stature could offer. Do you have greater power than…? That is the age old question. As the Creator of all things (Col. 1:16-17; Hebrews 1) Jesus initiated every other life to which He would later be compared. Yet, this objection is common by those who see the "great men" of religious history, and Jesus as one among many.

Jesus' answer was again direct and overt – I am not one among many. That is the **wrong conclusion**. I have the gift and the ability to deliver it. (4:13-14). It will surely accomplish satisfaction beginning within and flowing outward. It is superior to anything offered before, and it will deliver the ultimate and final rewards.

> **Distraction over Benefits**: The woman appeared to be ready to accept the offer made by Jesus, but Jesus knew she was not truly prepared. She was distracted by the part of the offer that appeared to care for her problems, but she did not comprehend what Jesus wanted from her (4:15).

From a Jewish perspective, there were three strikes against the woman at the well:

- She was a **WOMAN**. When Jesus' disciples returned, they "were surprised to find Him talking with a woman" (v. 27). For a Jewish man to speak to a woman in public was a definite breach of social custom. Many Jewish men would not even speak to their wives in public!

- She was a **SAMARITAN**. In Jesus' day, there was bitter hostility between Jews and Samaritans. . *Therefore the Samaritan woman said to Him, "How is it that You, being a Jew, ask me for a drink since I am a Samaritan woman?"* (v. 9).

The reason for the hostility of the Jews to the Samaritans goes back a long way. When the Assyrians took Samaria captive they deported large numbers of the inhabitants and replaced them by people from all over their empire (2 Kings 17:23-24). These people brought their own gods with them (2 Kings 17:29-31), but they added the worship of [the Lord] to their other practices (2 Kings 17:25, 28, 32-33, 41). In time their polytheism disappeared, and they worshiped [the Lord] alone, though their religion had its peculiarities. For example, they acknowledged as sacred scripture only the Pentateuch [Genesis through

Deuteronomy]. They thus cut themselves off from the riches in the Psalms, the Prophets, and other books. Their religion was also marked by a pronounced bitterness toward the Jews. When the Jews returned from exile in Babylon, the Samaritans offered to help them rebuild their temple, but the offer was refused (Ezra 4:2-3). This naturally engendered great bitterness. One might have expected that the Jews would have appreciated the fact that the Samaritans worshiped the same God as they did. But it did not work out this way. The Samaritans refused to worship at Jerusalem, preferring their own temple built on Mt. Gerizim c. 400 B.C. When this was burned by the Jews c. 128 B.C. relations between the two groups worsened. (Leon Morris, *The Gospel according to John*, pp. 226-27)

- She was **IMMORAL.** Jesus said to her, "You have correctly said, 'I have no husband'; for you have had five husbands, and the one whom you now have is not your husband." (v. 18). We are told that she arrived at the well at "the sixth hour" (v. 6). The sixth hour was noon. Women usually came in groups to collect water, either earlier or later in the day to avoid the sun's heat. But the Samaritan woman came alone at noon. Why? Perhaps her public shame caused her to be isolated from other women.

Jesus peeled into her life to help her expose the deep secret that she was hiding. He asked her to go and bring her husband. This was a respectful request, especially if she was about to make a bold move to accept His claims and follow Jesus (4:16). The woman replied, "I have no husband!" She told a half-truth (4:17-18). She was a woman who both lived in pain, and, as a result, walked in hidden compromise.

Here is the central issue – she wanted to add Jesus to a life of self-will and impure behaviors. That is a wrong assumption.

- It is true that Jesus loves us.
- It is true that He came to save us.
- It is simply NOT TRUE that He is so longing for us that He will simply dismiss our desire to continue to walk as we choose – in sinful practices that are forbidden by God.

I am not suggesting that we must become perfect to be saved – that is not even close to the truth. I am suggesting that Jesus is not interested in licensing wrong behaviors and adding salvation to our lives. If we assume this, we are not ready to truly receive Him – for we fail to understand the call to distinctiveness He demands.

Because we know that in the first century Jewish context, divorce was an issue of a man putting away a woman in most cases – it is likely that the woman's history of marriages has more to do with stinging repeated rejection and not simply a life as a "loose woman." She was evidently repeatedly judged deficient in some way by the men in her life. Rejection upon rejection appears to have left her desolate of self-respect. She eventually shed the need to even have the appearance of a real marriage (4:18).

Charles Swindoll, in his book *Growing Deep in the Christian Life*, tells the true story of a man who bought fried chicken dinners for himself and his girlfriend to enjoy on a picnic one afternoon. He was in for a surprise because the person behind the counter mistakenly gave him the wrong paper bag. Earlier, the manager had taken the money from the cash registers and placed it in an ordinary bag, hoping to disguise it on his way to the bank. But when the person working the cash register went to give the man his order, he grabbed the bag full of money instead of the bag full of chicken. Swindoll says, "After driving to their picnic site, the two of them sat down to enjoy some chicken. They discovered a whole lot more than chicken — over $800! But he was unusual. He quickly put the money back in the bag. They got back into the car and drove all the way back. Mr. Clean got out, walked in, and became an instant hero. By then, the manager was frantic. The guy with the bag of money looked the manager in the eye and said, 'I want you to know I came by to get a couple of chicken dinners and wound up with all this money here.' Well, the manager was thrilled to death. He said, 'Let me call the newspaper. I'm gonna have your picture put in the local paper. You're one of the most honest men I've ever heard of.' To which the man quickly responded, 'Oh, no. No, no, don't do that!' Then he leaned closer and whispered, 'You see, the woman I'm with is not my wife. She's, uh, somebody else's wife.'" Swindoll closes the story by saying, "Harder to find than lost cash is a perfect heart."

Our natural tendency is to cover up and conceal the truth. We hide the truth from ourselves and others. We put on our mask and go about our make-believe world. We play the pretender, just as the woman at the well did with Jesus. She presented another self to Jesus, the one she wanted him to see, and hid her true self.

Theological Redirection: Jesus spoke resounding truth into the life of the woman, and she knew it. He opened her eyes to the truth about her own pain. He peeled her heart to its core. She perceived He was a prophet. Yet, she was not ready to surrender to Jesus. She re-directed the conversation to theology and arguments over the place and nature of worship, emphasizing the difference between Jews and Samaritans (4:19-20). Some read these words and believe she is just cleaning up loose ends, but I believe there was a very basic smokescreen she was attempting to raise. It is always preferable to redirect the painful peering into the hurt soul by the Lord to a theological discussion. Theology can easily be a cold discussion – removed of self-inspection and the pain of inner reflection -- and Jesus was hitting very close to her center.

Jesus answered her and told her that she was essentially on the **wrong issue**. She was concerned with the PLACE of worship, and Jesus answered with the NATURE of worship (4:21-24). Jesus flatly claimed that neither mountain would last, nor the worship systems found on them wouldn't last either. Worship is neither a service nor a hall. Jesus foretold that both would be swallowed up in the larger truth – worship would one day be both spirit empowered from within the believer and centered on the truth that was revealed by God's Word. Getting caught up in any discussion that kept the pressure on the woman to yield her broken heart to the Lord, no matter the value of the discussion, was a distraction.

This is so amazing because Jesus' method of confronting this woman would be scorned in this day when no one is really right and no one is really wrong. We say, "Everyone has their own truth, and we should respect that by not trying to change the way they think or believe." Our **culture asserts that truth is whatever you sincerely believe in**. But Jesus **did not affirm the woman's error, he pointed her to the truth**. He bluntly told her that the Samaritans were worshiping what they did not know. He told her that everything she had believed all her life had been wrong. He said, "Salvation is from the Jews." She was uncomfortable and thought she would change the subject again.

The Voice of Procrastination: "Someday I hope it will happen for me!" was the final objection raised (4:25). Many have raised it. "One of these days, when things work out for me, then I will be ready to commit to Jesus."

Jesus replied to the woman, "You are on the wrong timing!" The time for her salvation was the day Jesus beckoned. Later would be too late. The acceptable time of salvation was the day of the presentation. Jesus, the very Anointed of God was standing before her. Today was the day she needed to respond. That future time she pondered and dreamed of was no longer relevant.

Perhaps you relate to the woman. Maybe you have heard that Jesus will save you from your sins, but you possess the "**Doubt of Intention**" – you aren't sure what He will expect you to lay on the line to follow Him.

Maybe you have been hurt by people that pressed into your heart the idea that you are worthless. You may suffer from the "**Sense of Unworthiness**" – the notion that you must clean up first to invite Jesus within.

Maybe you are awaiting some new proof that sets apart Jesus from other great religious leaders. You have the "**Doubt of His Ability**" – and await Him to show you the truth.

Could it be that at some time in the past you were ready to accept Jesus to get salvation, but you didn't intend to give your life to Him – you had "**Distraction over Benefits**" – and wanted to simply add Jesus without surrendering anything. You were not saved.

Maybe some argument of theology is keeping you from clearly hearing the message that you are lost. Maybe you are worried about what version of the Bible you should read, or how baptism truly works and why people you know disagree. You are being tempted to "**Theological Redirection**" – when EVERY decent translation says that you need to yield, and everyone says that baptism isn't the issue. (The thief on the cross knew better!)

Maybe you have thought about coming to Christ "some day" but offer nothing but the "**Voice of Procrastination**" that someday it will happen for you. Can you really put this off? Are you so secure in your driving, in your body and its health, in everyone around you and your own safety that you KNOW you can wait?

In order to bring about healing in the lives of others, we must first learn to become lovers of the unlovable.

I want to tell you the story of **Ted Stallard** - a young man who was turned off by school. Very sloppy in appearance. Expressionless. Unattractive. Slow. Often times he would simply sit in class and stare off into space, unresponsive, which was an irritation to his teacher. Miss Thompson enjoyed bearing down her red pen -- as she placed big red X's beside his many wrong answers. If only she had studied Ted's school records more carefully. They read:

> 1st grade: Ted shows promise with his work and attitude, but (has) poor home situation.
> 2nd grade: Ted could do better. Mother seriously ill. Receives little help from home.
> 3rd grade: Ted is a good boy but too serious. He is a slow learner. His mother died this year.
> 4th grade: Ted is very slow, but well-behaved. His father shows no interest whatsoever.

Christmas arrived. The children piled elaborately wrapped gifts on their teacher's desk. Ted brought one too. It was wrapped in brown paper and held together with Scotch Tape. Miss Thompson opened each gift as the children crowded around to watch. Out of Ted's package fell a gaudy rhinestone bracelet, with half of the stones missing, and a bottle of cheap perfume. The children began to snicker. But she silenced them by splashing some of the perfume on her wrist, and letting them smell it. She put the bracelet on too. At day's end, after the other children had left, Ted came by the teacher's desk and said, "Miss Thompson, you smell just like my mother. And the bracelet looks real pretty on you. I'm glad you like my presents." He left. Miss Thompson got down on her knees and asked God to forgive her and to change her attitude. The next day, the children were greeted by a reformed teacher -- one committed to loving each of them. Especially the slow ones. Especially Ted.

Surprisingly -- or maybe, not surprisingly, Ted began to show great improvement. He actually caught up with most of the students and even passed a few. Graduation came and went. Miss Thompson heard nothing from Ted for a long time.

Then, one day, she received this note: Dear Miss Thompson: I wanted you to be the first to know. I will be graduating second in my class. Love, Ted

Four years later, another note arrived:
Dear Miss Thompson: They just told me I will be graduating first in my class. I wanted you to be first to know. The university has not been easy, but I liked it. Love, Ted

And four years later:
Dear Miss Thompson: As of today, I am Theodore Stallard, M.D. How about that? I wanted you to be the first to know. I am getting married next month, the 27th to be exact. I want you to come and sit where my mother would sit if she were alive. You are the only family I have now; Dad died last year. Love, Ted

Miss Thompson attended that wedding, and sat where Ted's mother would have sat. The compassion she had shown that young man entitled her to that privilege.

Every day we come in contact with people like Ted. However, for some, the hurt doesn't always show on the outside. Some people wear a mask to cover the invisible pain that exists just beneath the surface of their lives. It may be your next door neighbor - a member of your family - a spouse - a friend - the person sitting next to you right now. It is that private pain that they live with every day: it eats away at their soul. The pain is often caused by sin, and failure.

If we would only realize just how much healing we could bring about in the lives of these broken-hearted, hurting people - those that the world, and sadly some Christians, call the unlovable.

If we would only learn to respond to their hurt with love and not condemnation, like Jesus did.

When we are confronted with the direction that Jesus offers, we often place roadblock objections - but Jesus knows the answers to deal with our objections.

Knowing Jesus
Lessons in the Gospel of John

Lesson Seven: John 4:27-42 "The 'Wax On, Wax Off' Discipleship School"

It was all the way back in 1984, that Mr. Miyagi taught his pupil in "The Karate Kid" a series of lessons by making him do practical projects. What Mr. Miyagi did for his student was plagiarize a discipleship method that was used by Jesus extensively nearly 2000 years before. Jesus sent the disciples into a Samaritan village to get some food for the group, while He encountered a badly treated and scorned woman at the city well. When the disciples returned from the village with the food, they came upon Jesus ending a discussion with the woman. The whole scene was a "wax on, wax off" teaching moment. Jesus used the opportunity to teach **seven lessons** to mature the men that were following Him.

Key Principle: We, as disciples, are shaped to maturity by the "planned experiences" God takes us through, but we must carefully observe the lessons!

Seven Lessons toward Maturity:

Lesson One: True satisfaction comes when we fulfill the purpose for which we were created. (4:31-34)

- This satisfaction is not comprehended by the new believer, but is learned by maturity in Messiah (cp. 4:32).
- The satisfaction comes through the faithful execution of the call from God (4:34a)
- Satisfaction also comes through the completion of a project within the call (4:34b).

*John 4:31 Meanwhile, the disciples were urging Him, saying, "Rabbi, eat." 32 But He said to them, "**I have food** to eat that you do not know about." 33 So the disciples were saying to one another, "No one brought Him anything to eat, did he?" 34 Jesus said to them, "My food is **to do the will of Him who sent Me** and to **accomplish** His work."*

John Piper has said, "God is most glorified in us when we are most satisfied in Him."

God designed the human machine to run on **Himself**. He Himself is the fuel our spirits were designed to burn, or the food our spirits were designed to feed on. There is no other. That is why it is just no good asking God to make us happy in our own way without bothering about religion. **God cannot give us a happiness and peace apart from Himself, because it is not there.** There is no such thing. (C.S. Lewis, *Mere Christianity*)

It may take some detours to understand what your call is, but you MUST seek God about why He created you where He did, when He did. YOU ARE NOT AN ACCIDENT and you may not get it right the first time!

The year was **1920**. The scene was the **examining board for selecting missionaries**. Standing before the board was a young man named **Oswald Smith**. One dream dominated his heart. He wanted to be a missionary. Over and over again, he prayed, "Lord, I want to go as a missionary for you. Open a door of service for me." Now, at last, his prayer would be answered. When the examination was over, the board turned Oswald Smith down. He did not meet their qualifications. He failed the test. Oswald Smith had set his direction, but now life gave him a detour. What would he do? **As Oswald Smith prayed, God planted another idea in his heart. If he could not go as a missionary, he would build a church which could send out missionaries**. And that is what he did. Oswald Smith pastored The People's Church in Toronto, Canada, which **sent out more missionaries than any other church at that time**. Oswald Smith brought God into the situation, and God transformed his detour into a main thoroughfare of service. (Brian L. Harbour, *Rising Above the Crowd*)

Lesson Two: The mature believer sees a harvest where others see a way to help themselves. (John 4:35)

The disciples encountered the same people in the village that Jesus did, and the woman who returned to her village did – yet the disciples yielded only physical fruit (a meal) and not spiritual fruit (souls). Why? Because they could not see the people as they were – needy and open to the good news.

*John 4:35 Do you not say, "There are yet four months, and then comes the harvest?" Behold, I say to you, "Lift up your eyes and look on the fields, that **they are white for harvest**."*

William Booth started the Salvation Army. But what led him to do that? Here's the story: One night he couldn't sleep and went for a walk thru the slums of London. The rain was beating down that night on the derelicts asleep on the street, and it broke his heart. He went home and when his wife asked where he had been he replied, "I've been to Hell." He saw the homeless as more than just drunks and losers, and remembered they were once somebody's baby, and used to be loved, and rather than blame them for their condition and keep walking, he decided that night to do something about it, and give them another chance to make something of themselves. **His organization was started with the idea of giving the homeless a hand up, not just a handout.** Sure, many turn around and return to their old ways, but compassion made way for thousands to be saved and their lives changed!

A great many will not see what you see, even if they are qualified to see, and even if they are standing right next to you! You must see, and you must respond to what the Lord shows you!

The *Times-Reporter* of New Philadelphia, Ohio, reported in September, 1985 a celebration of a New Orleans municipal pool. The party around the pool was held to celebrate the first summer in memory without a drowning at the New Orleans city pool. In honor of the occasion, 200 people gathered, including 100 certified lifeguards. As the party was breaking up and the four lifeguards on duty began to clear the pool, they found a fully dressed body in the deep end. They tried to revive Jerome Moody, 31, but it was too late. He had drowned surrounded by lifeguards celebrating their successful season. (*Times-Reporter*, September 1985)

Jesus said: "They are white for harvest!" What the Lord said to His disciple is a very important passage in the Bible, especially to all mission-minded local Churches of today.

- Indifference is a fruit of questionable philosophy
- Indifference blunts our awareness
- Indifference blurs our spiritual vision
- Indifference obscures our way to success
- Indifference subdues our real purpose
- Indifference robs our opportunities
- Indifference provokes our hearts to go astray

We must look again to see the big difference we can make when we respond to what the Lord shows us. The mission field isn't just far away; it is also in OUR COUNTRY...

From a "Church-culture" to a "Mission-field" (Kennon Callahan): Did you know since **1991**, the adult population in the United States has grown by **15%**? During that same period the number of adults who **do not attend church has nearly doubled**, rising from **39 million to 75 million – a 92% increase**!

- The United States is the **third largest unchurched nation** in the world.

- North America is the **only continent where Christianity is not growing**.
- The United States is now the **13th largest receptor** of Christian missionaries in the world.
- Only **4 percent of Americans** have a biblical worldview.
- More than 80 percent of all churches in the United States are plateaued or declining.
    - We lose 72 churches per week or 10.27 per day. We gain 24 churches per week or 3.42 per day. That's a net loss of 48 churches per week or 6.85 per day.
- Half of all churches last year did not add one new member through conversion growth.
- While the U.S. population grew by 11.4 percent over the last 10 years, church growth declined by 9.5 percent fifty years. In other words, we are not even reaching our children. George Barna.
- By the year 2010, more than 100 million Americans will look elsewhere than church for spiritual direction.
- Evangelical churches have failed to gain an additional two percent of the American population in the past
- The church to population ratio is also declining for every 10,000 Americans…

    - In 1900 there were 27 churches for every 10,000 Americans.
    - In 1950 there were 17 churches for every 10,000 Americans.
    - In 1996 there were 11 churches for every 10,000 Americans.

Lesson Three: Those who see the field and do the work will reap the harvest for all of us, while <u>others remain oblivious</u> to the field <u>until</u> the harvest comes in. (4:36)

John 4:36 Already he who reaps is receiving wages and is gathering fruit for life eternal; so that he who sows and he who reaps may rejoice together.

Stop and think: Much that we reap, we never planted. Somebody else did and we reap the consequences. Sometimes we reap things that are good, but not always. Let's look at the positive side first. We receive many blessings given to us by God for which we have performed no labor whatever. In fact, the Lord wants us to trust Him that He will provide all of our needs even as He provides for the birds of the air (Matthew 6:25-34).

The Lord extends His blessings to all men as "He makes his sun to rise on the evil and on the good, and sends rain on the just and on the unjust" (Matthew 5:45).

Do you remember the amazing rescue of the nine miners trapped in the Quecreek mine in Pennsylvania in July of 2002? They were trapped 240 feet beneath the surface for a total of 77 hours. I recall staying up into the early morning hours and watching on that final day as they were hauled out of the darkness to safety one-by-one. But the rescue was anything but easy. A drill bit broke in the rescue shaft they had started to drill. They couldn't get the broken pieces out so after a new one was flown in they had to start another shaft. Communications was disrupted for a while and the miners themselves almost gave up and wrote notes to their loved ones. **Their rescue was the result of a coordinated effort by hundreds.** I remember cheering and stopping to thank God when they were finally rescued. **God says that there is the same response over one sinner who repents** (See Luke 15:3-10).

When a lost one comes to Christ, there is great reason to rejoice together!

It reminds me of the converted cannibal on a South Sea Island was sitting by a large pot reading his Bible. An anthropologist saw him and was curious as to what he was doing. He approached the native and said, "What are you doing?" The cannibal replied, "**I'm reading the Bible**." Upset that a "western book" would destroy the culture of the man, the anthropologist then said, "Don't you know that modern man has rejected that book?" The cannibal looked him over and said, "Sir, if it weren't for this book, you'd be in that pot."

The story goes that Mark Twain loved to go fishing, but he hated to catch fish. The problem was he went fishing to relax, and **catching fish ruined his relaxation**, since he had to take the fish off the hook and do something with it. When he wanted to relax by doing nothing, people thought he was lazy, but if he went fishing he could relax all he wanted. People would see him sitting by the river bank and they would say, "**Look, he's fishing, don't bother him**." So Mark Twain had the perfect solution: **he would take a fishing pole, line, and a bobber, but he wouldn't put a hook on the end**. He would cast the bobber in the water and lay back on the bank. That way he could relax all he wanted and he would be bothered neither by man nor fish.

Mark Twain is like a lot of Christians I know. They have their pole in the water, but there is no hook on the end. They are not fishing; they are relaxing.

> **Lesson Four: The mature disciple will not allow the amazement with Jesus to wane in his life, and cannot help but share.** (4:36)

The woman was new to Jesus and His message, but she was moved to share and sowed her newfound amazement (perhaps faith?). The disciples were deeply familiar with Jesus, but the novelty had worn off, and they simply didn't share that He was near the village!

Evangelism is a program to un-amazed disciples. Those who are struck by the presence of Jesus need not force to share their excitement.

John 4:37 For in this case the saying is true, 'One sows and another reaps.'

People treat evangelism like it is an unusual thing, like it is something that should be a meeting or an organized trip. They don't get it. When I am amazed at Jesus it is natural to talk about Him. When I am not really walking in His love, it is a strain. They don't get it!

Like Carl Boyle, the sales representative, who was driving home through his suburban neighborhood one day when he saw a group of young children selling Kool-Aid on a corner. They had taped the typical hand-scrawled sign on their stand: "Kool-Aid, 10 cents." As a salesman, Carl was intrigued. He pulled over to the curb, and one of the boys came up to his car and asked if he would like strawberry or grape Kool-Aid. Carl placed his order and handed the boy a quarter. After much deliberation, the children determined he had some change coming, and rifled through the old box in which they kept their money, until they finally came up with the correct amount. The boy returned with the change, then stood by the side of the car watching him as he drank. The boy became impatient and asked if Carl was finished drinking. "Just about," said Carl, "Why?" **"That's the only cup we have," answered the boy, "and we need it to stay in business.** Some people get only PART of what they need to get!**

Three men are hiking and they come upon a large raging river. They need to get to the other side, but they don't know how. The first man says, "God, give me the strength to cross this river." Poof! God gives him big arms and strong legs, and he swims across the raging river. It takes him two hours, but he makes it. Seeing this, the second man prays, "God, give me the **STRENGTH** . . . and the **TOOLS** . . . to cross this river." Poof! God gives him a rowboat, and he rows across the raging river. It takes him 90 minutes, but he makes it. Seeing this, the third man says, "God, give me the strength and the tools and the **INTELLIGENCE** . . . to cross this river." And poof! **God turns him into a woman. She looks at the map, hikes upstream for 50 yards, and then walks across the bridge!** (SOURCE: from a sermon by Marc Axelrod, SermonCentral.com, *God the Rebuilder,* 6/30/08)

What is the transformation you need to see the harvest and get into the reaping business? It is the amazement with an awesome Savior!

> **Lesson Five: Mature disciples understand they do not reap the harvest on their own – it is a work aided and seeded by many**. (4:38-39)

Jesus said, "I sent you to get food you didn't grow, but you were blessed by the working hands of others. You understood that. You knew I didn't expect you to buy the field, plant it, reap it, grind the flour and make the bread. You could simply purchase and enjoy what another labored over."

Spiritually speaking, you must learn that you gain a harvest because of the labor of many others.

John 4:38 "I sent you to reap that for which you have not labored; others have labored and you have entered into their labor." 39 From that city many of the Samaritans believed in Him because of the word of the woman who testified, "He told me all the things that I have done."

Patrick Johnstone wrote the monumental world prayer guide, *Operation World,* including notes about the most encouraging evangelical developments in the 21st Century:

"**Accelerated growth:** Since the 1990's, the Evangelical movement **grew faster than ever before**, according to our massive database of detailed research reaching back to the 1960's. **Only 6.3% of the world's population lives in a culture without a witnessing local**. Of the 28% (2.7 billion) of the world un-reached peoples, only 2% has no local witness at all. 4.3% is left without a resident witness to the people group and 22% are left without an indigenous church.

"**The AD 2000 movement:** The AD 2000 movement was the most effective and best-targeted global network for promoting world missions which ever existed. It helped initiate church planting projects among un-reached people groups, created synergy in the Body of Christ and was instrumental in the birth of many missions' initiatives. The challenge to all congregations and agencies to adopt people groups for prayer and ministry gained momentum since the 1990s. **Progress was logged for the 1583 peoples listed in the Joshua Project list for Oct 2000 with the following results.** There was a reported church planting team in **1084 of the people groups of the 1583 targeted and evidence of a congregation of 100 members in 487.** This **does not include the possible 2000 people groups under 10,000 in population** that remain inadequately researched and may need pioneer work. Praise God for these achievements and pray for the momentum to increase.

"**The collapse of the Iron Curtain:** The collapse of the Iron Curtain and the end of the USSR created completely new opportunities for mission in Central Asia.

"**Thousands of Muslims turn to Jesus:** More than ever before, Muslims turned to Jesus: Northern African Berbers, Jordanians, Bosnians and Afghanis. The attack on the World Trade Center on 11th September 2001 could be a key moment for a divided Islamic world looking for an alternative belief system.

"**China's Christianity:** Starting with only 4 million Christians in 1949, the **Body of Christ in China grew to over 90 million** by the year 2000. The development of truly indigenous forms of Christianity, despite growing persecution at the end of the 1990's, is one of the most important factors in 21st Century Christianity.

"**The astonishing and mostly undocumented growth of the church in India:** The official numbers (2.34% Christians in 1991) are far lower than the truth, deliberately hiding the true extent of Christianity in the nation. The true figures are certainly far more than double, and look like only the beginning. The 'untouchable' Dalits have started leaving Hinduism, which could lead to an immense growth of Indian churches. **Gospel for Asia reports it has 14,000 full time church planters out seeing approximately ten new churches started every week**. They are now starting to broadcast Christian programming on TV throughout India in addition to their radio broadcasts.

"**Christian media's decisive contribution:** Christian media have changed the faith and world view of millions. Significant examples are the **Jesus Film**, satellite television such as SAT7 in the Arab world, Christian radio in China and India and the explosive growth of interest in using the Internet for evangelization and discipleship. The *Jesus Film* has had **4.1 billion people view it** and has yielded **128 million inquirers**. The goal is also in translating the script of the *Jesus Film* into every language spoken by 50,000 people was virtually achieved by 2001. Well over 99% of the world population would be able to view the film in a language they know.

Christian radio can reach approximately 99% of the world's population. This has practically meant that weekly broadcasts in 372 mega-languages are done each week. IN the 1990's 115 languages were added leaving only 164 with no broadcasts. It is estimated that the potential audience is now 99% (assuming good radio reception, availability of radios and power and the interest in seeking the correct frequencies)."(Source: www.gmi.org , www.operationworld.org)

Lesson Six: The believer that loves the lost will reach the lost. (4:40-41)

The woman identified with the people as "her people." Jesus dwelt with the Samaritans to show them love and care -- the disciples had no real love for the people (cp. Lk. 9:54).

*John 4:40 So when the Samaritans came to Jesus, they were asking Him to stay with them; and He **stayed there two days**. 41 Many more believed because of His word;*

A pastor friend wrote: In Bible college I went on weekend ministry extension to a local apartment complex, the Sunrise Apartments in a poverty stricken area of Pensacola, FL. A friend and I started the Sunrise Bible Club and went out each Saturday morning. We didn't have to knock on many doors before word spread, and kids would run out to the courtyard each week to play games with us, have story time, and many got saved. During game time there wasn't enough of us to go around. The kids said, "Swing me next," "Carry me on your shoulders," but I'll never forget the little girl Crystal--she didn't want to play, but waited in line for attention, and when it was her turn said, "Hold me!" I picked her up, and was taken aback by how firmly she squeezed me, like she didn't want me to ever put her down. Then she said, "Love me!"

Lesson Seven: People may begin by following the believer, but in the end it comes down to them accepting the Word of the Savior! (4:42)

John 4:42 and they were saying to the woman, "It is no longer because of what you said that we believe, for we have heard for ourselves and know that this One is indeed the Savior of the world."

God uses us to get His Word to them out of love for US. He could do it without, but He chooses to allow us to participate in the redemption process!

The disciple is shaped to maturity by the "planned experiences" God takes them through, but we must carefully observe the lessons! We must be careful not to simply use the time on this planet to "fill out our needs". We must observe the people around us, the specific places God places us - and look for a way to bring Him joy through our lives!

Knowing Jesus
Lessons in the Gospel of John

Lesson Eight: John 4:46-54 "Long Distance Healing"

Man can blast other men to the moon or up to a space station. We can engineer DNA strands in a "Petrie dish." We can store 100,000 pages of text on a silicon chip the size of a fingertip. We can explore the depths of the ocean with an unmanned submarine and fly a mission thousands of miles away from an unmanned drone to shoot a missile at a small group of men near a cave.

Much of what we can do most of us cannot truly understand.

- What does "**faith**" really mean in a time like ours?
- What does it look like to truly **believe**?
- Do we trust the word of Jesus so fully that we change our daily life to conform to what He says is true?

Ever since I was young I have heard people say that I just needed to "accept some things by faith" as if this was the end point when something could not be explained.

- Yet, is that w**hat God intended me to do?**
- **Is faith simply the last refuge cop-out for things that Christians** don't know or haven't searched out?
- Am I supposed to turn off my mind and simply trust whatever I am told about God that cannot seem to be explained?

In the *Bible*, faith is not about whether you can explain the "how" of something or not. Faith, in essence, is the absolute trust that the world is not how it appears, but how God says it is in His Word. It is a "biblical world view." When I accept Jesus by faith, I accept that God's record of Who Jesus is and what He did was both correct and accepted by the Creator. When I walk by faith I walk in the light of His Word and see the world as He proclaims it to be.

Key Principle: I truly believe God's Word only when I accept the Word as it is stated and change my life to conform to what it says I should do and become.

The story recorded in John's Gospel (4:46-54) is a profound and yet simple story. The entire story is built upon the details of time and distance between two ancient villages of the Galilee. I have walked the path between these villages, and though neither is a living town today, the ruins still mark the places. The steep slope of the incline from Capernaum up the Arbel pass to ancient Khirbet Cana is no less than an arduous eight hour journey. That same path in reverse direction is a mere five and one half hours journey.

Let's drop in as an observer to the happenings in Cana some two thousand years ago… The text can be broken into **three** simple **parts**:

- The Encounter with Jesus (4:46-50a).
- The Trust in Jesus (4:50b-52).
- The Full Grasp of Belief (4:53-54).

First, we need to examine the "encounter with Jesus." (4:46-50a)

A desperate man grasped at the reputation of Jesus based on His previous work (4:46-47).

We know **four things** about the man:

- The man knew of Jesus. (4:46a)
- He knew what others claimed He could do. (4:46a)

- The man was faced with a heart rending problem he could not care for. (4:46b)

In this way we say that problems are often friends and companions that lead us on the path to the Lord. They break down our self-sufficiency. They unmask our vulnerability.

Desperation opens our hearts to make us willing to take our need to Jesus and abandon self-reliance.

The man had to traverse both the twenty miles from Capernaum to Cana and the humility of the social difference in status between Jesus and himself. The nobleman had to lower himself to seek help from a humble Jewish villager and iterant preacher. There is no home into which sickness and sorrow cannot enter – and when it does, it reduces the imposed social divisions between us.

C.S. Lewis reminds: "God speaks to us in our health but he shouts to us in our pain." Crisis led him to Jesus. Crisis reduces our arrogance and airs and allows us to kneel.

- The man reached out for Jesus and begged Him to have mercy and deliver him from the clutches of the terrible need. (John 4:47)

Jesus responded in two ways:

- Jesus told those about that Galileans only seemed to believe what they could SEE. John (4:48)

Jesus' reaction does not seem loving at all – but almost heartless and cold. He says (apparently to the crowd around Him): "Unless you people see miraculous signs and wonders you will never believe."

Why take a seemingly desperate man and hold out on him like that? The answer is not as complicated as it may appear.

This is another story to show that Jesus knows the heart of man (John 2:24-25). He knew how manipulative people can be. We will move Heaven and Earth to achieve what we want. When the miracle is something as pure as healing for a child or when God's intervention is something else, but when it's done there is no commitment to Him or His message, **we use God to get what we want rather than allow the struggle to lead us to full submission to God**.

This passage helps us to examine God's objective with troubles in our lives. People say: "If God is a healer, then why are there sick children in the world? If God is peaceful, then why do wars happen? If God is loving, then why do bad things happen to good people?" Behind these questions there is the desire to **see God prove Himself by taking these evil things away** so that we will all believe in Him and live happily ever after.
The problem then is not submission based on what He has done, but God having left Himself cloaked because He refused to do what was necessary to make us able to believe.

The problem is based on false logic.

Think about it: There are plenty who have enough to eat, aren't struggling with the effects of war, plenty who have food on the table and a roof over their heads. Yet plenty of those people do not have a relationship with God. There have been many good times in our lives that did not yield surrendered lives. **Our relationship with God cannot be simply based on His ability to heal us or perform other miracles for us. Our faith must leave this world's way of thinking and take on a biblical world view, solely based on surrender to the Word of Jesus.**

Why didn't Jesus make it easy for the man? In our modern American lifestyle, we often act as though life should be easy. Ease, in fact is not always what is best for us. **A faith that requires no effort is a faith that is not worth having.** Faith takes effort because it requires a change on our part. It comes from God, Ephesians tells us – and not ourselves. Yet, it comes to those who persevere and put forth the effort to surrender to Jesus' role in our lives. **A new king sits upon the throne only after a pitted struggle removed the former king!**

- Jesus told the man that he could trust the Word alone – your son is made well. (4:50a)

The man changed when he encountered Jesus:

- At first, he was clearly panicked by the delay and distance (things he could observe with his eyes and heart) and tried to get Jesus to understand the immediacy of the need (4:49).

There's an old story about a traveler in the early days of the west. When he came to a large river, he discovered there was no bridge. Fortunately it was winter and the great river was sheeted over with ice. But the traveler was afraid to trust himself to it, not knowing how thick it was. Finally with infinite caution, he crept on his hands and knees and managed to get halfway over. And then he heard--yes he heard singing from behind. Cautiously he turned, and there, out of the dusk, came another traveler, driving a four-horse load of coal over the ice, singing as he went!

- After Jesus spoke, he clearly believed the word so thoroughly that he exchanged panic for trust (50b). How do I know? Let's take a closer look…

Second, we need to examine the "trust in Jesus." (4:50b-52)

Jesus spoke to the man at one o'clock (the seventh hour of the daylight - 4:52b) and yet he did not return the same day. The text is clear the man encountered his slaves "the next day." How could this be? He came with panic in his heart and yet stayed from one o'clock in the afternoon until the next day to journey down the five and one half hour path to his home? **The key to the change is the word "BELIEVED" in verse 50.**

The man *believed*. The man *trusted* the **word** of Jesus. He exchanged the view of the distance and the difficulty in curing his sick child at such a great distance with the whole-hearted trust in what Jesus told him – "Your son is alive and well." He rested in that promise overnight. He ceased striving to find a way to care for the need because he believed the need was already met.

It was in his **going, not in his arriving** that he received the assurance that his faith had been rewarded. **A single ACT of faith led to a LIFE of faith.** In Genesis 12 God called Abraham to follow Him from his home to new land that he had never seen. His decision is described in Hebrews 12:8, **"he went out, not knowing."**

Here is the key: I truly believe God's Word only when I accept the Word as it is stated and change my life to conform to what it says I should do and become. I change my behavior. I rest in the words and see life through them. I don't keep seeing as others see!

Third, we need to offer some comment to the "full grasp of belief." (4:53-54)

Two important expansions occurred in the heart of the man after his initial trust was confirmed by the facts on the ground:

- The man trusted in Jesus' words, but that trust was confirmed in his life *as he walked* in those words (4:53).
- The seed of belief became a **testimony** that when shared sprung up in a tree that sheltered the whole family, and they all believed together (4:53b).

A testimony can produce great faith.

C.S. Lewis wrote, "I have to believe that Jesus was (and is) God. And it seems plain as a matter of history that He taught His followers that the new life was communicated in this way. In other words, I believe it on His authority. Ninety-nine percent of the things you believe are believed on authority... The ordinary person believes in the solar system, atoms, and the circulation of the blood on authority--because the scientists say so. Every historical statement is believed on authority. None of us has seen the Norman Conquest or the defeat of the Spanish Armada. But we believe them simply because people who did see them have left writings that tell us about them." (C.S. Lewis, *A Grief Observed*)

As we examine the story then, **what is faith**? Faith is seeing the world as God says it is, not as my eyes say it is. My senses are limited to a faulty view of the situation.

The other day I was driving and I wanted to make a left on Thunderbird Road coming from The Home Depot. My wife was in the car and it was raining. I looked first to my left – no one was coming. I looked to my right – no one was coming... or so I thought. I began to pull out and my wife said, "Stop, stop! There's a car!" Blocked by a blind spot on the car at that angle and by my wife's lovely head, I totally missed the view of the car. I was responding to what I saw, but not what was truly there. I was boldly proceeding as if I knew what was there, but I did not truly see things as they were.

Faith is the ability to see the truth. Since Jesus is the truth, and speaks the truth – it is the ability to see "through His eyes".

Akin to **faith** is the biblical word "**BELIEVE**" (επιστευσεν from pisteuo: to have faith in, upon, or with respect to, a person or thing, to entrust). The idea is only truly seen in change (as James notes). **It is "the convincing of the mind and heart that leads to a willful surrender to the conditions of that truth accepted."** When Abraham believed that God would send him a son -he built a nursery. The belief was not complete until the actions accompanied the faith confirmed the change in authority over the life of the man of faith.

Sometimes, **it even takes time to find out if the surrender is real**:

A young woman had become critically ill and her prognosis was grim; she would likely die within the year. Her family had a nominal "Easter and Christmas" commitment to the church, so the discussions in the hospital between this young pastor and the family always ploughed new ground. The woman challenged him – if Jesus healed in the *Bible*, he should be able to heal me today. If not, what use was He? So she begged and bargained. "If only" God would show mercy, the family urged, they would completely recommit themselves and come to church every Sunday. This earnest young pastor prayed with all his heart. He refused to join the ranks of those who said, "If it is thy will." It was God's will that she be healed, he concluded. Then to his amazement, God healed her—completely. And with the physicians shaking their heads, she was sent home from the hospital. Next Sunday, the entire family was there in the front pew, dressed and sparkling. The young woman gave her testimony, praising God for His goodness. The following Sunday, the family was there again. In four weeks, it was only the woman and her husband. And after that, attendance was sporadic until they dropped into their previous pattern. Before long, the woman rationalized the entire incident. She had experienced the most dramatic sign God could give her: healing, bathed in prayer and surrounded by the church. But after only two months, its power dimmed to nothing. (source: sermon central illustrations)

Her surrender was not real, though her amazement was. She was amazed at first that God could and would act on her behalf. If our encounter is with amazement alone, it will fade. If our encounter led us to true surrender – we will ever be changed and marked by our walk with Jesus. **Jesus is looking for surrender to Him**, not an applause line from an amazed admirer.

Jean Francois Gravelet, the great Blondin, was the first tightrope walker to appear at Niagara Falls. On June 30, 1859 the rope was in position and at five o'clock in the afternoon Blondin started the trip that was to make history. As he began his ascent toward the Canadian shore, he paused, steadied the balancing pole and suddenly executed a back somersault. Never content merely to repeat his last performance, Blondin crossed his rope on a bicycle, walked blindfolded, pushed a wheelbarrow, cooked an omelet in the center, and made the trip with his hands and feet manacled. And then, he announced that on August 19 he would cross the gorge carrying his manager, Harry Colcord, on his back. (source: http://www.niagara-info.com/historic.htm)

Harry Culcord had demonstrated biblical belief. He didn't just have the faith to know that Blondin could make the trip, he acted on that faith in belief. In that same way, Jesus invites us to crawl upon His back, and to surrender control to Him for our lives and future. Nothing less will do. (source: sermon central illustrations)

I truly believe God's Word only when I accept the Word as it is stated and change my life to conform to what it says I should do and become.

Knowing Jesus: Lessons in the Gospel of John (I)

Knowing Jesus
Lessons in the Gospel of John

Lesson Nine: John 5: 1-47 "How to Start a Religion and Kill Real Faith"

Some people love the **rules** and want to make everyone around them do them, but they don't really care about the **people, nor** do they really have a love and **intimacy** with God. They are **great at religion and lousy at faith**.

- **Faith is about seeing things as God says they are,** and becoming what you know God made you to be.

- **Religion is about making people conform** to what you believe they ought to be.

- **Faith has rules, but they are based on true caring.**

- **Religion is based on true control.**

Which one are we trying to build? Will people around us be able to tell?

Key Principle: Jesus called His followers to be people of FAITH not RELIGION. People of faith love lost people and want to walk daily and deeply with God.

The Setting: (5:1-7)

> **The Point in time** (5:1). After the victories in Samaria (John 4) and the Galilee long distance healing (4:46ff) Jesus headed with some followers to Jerusalem. The feast is not specified, but is likely Passover (Pesach), Pentecost (Shavuot), or Tabernacles (Sukkot) as specified in Deuteronomy 16:16.

The Place in town (5:2-4). North of the Temple Mount where the ridge sets higher on the former property of the Zatha family, a pool was cut several hundred years before our story. The water entered by both the surface and some submerged vents that caused the stirring of the water. The "probatic" pools were beside the sheep market, and what was possibly a former Greek shrine from which the healings were reported in a superstitious way.

The Participant in Trouble (5:5-7).

Three truths are shared about the man Jesus encountered:

- The man was **sick** for a long time (5:5). The man appeared to be ill with a long term effect of suffering the inability to walk (as-then'-i-ah: feebleness of mind or body). According to Jesus' conversation with the man after his healing, the illness was because of some sin in his life that the man was fully aware of (5:14: sin no more is may-ket'-ee: no further -- any longer).
- The man was **quiet** – not begging (5:6).
- The man was un-noticed by others around him and felt **alone** (5:7).

The Miracle: (5:8-9)

The Need broken (5:8-9): The man had NO ONE, but was able to obey Jesus ON HIS OWN. The sin that bound the man crushed his life and left him alone and broken (cp. 5:14). The man knew what the problem was. When Jesus encountered the man, He asked the man if he was ready to surrender yet. When the man cried, "I will, but I need help!" Jesus offered the only thing he needed to be helped – the Word of Jesus. The man added obedience and the deal was complete (5:9).

The Problem: (5:10-16):

> The man followed the Word of Jesus, but that word was not the common idea of the day. People who had tripped across the man for thirty-eight years, not offering to assist him when the water stirred, suddenly became interested in him when he didn't do what they thought he was to do. They never cared before, but now HE was the center of attention. 5:10 doesn't say they were religious leaders… just people that were nearby - those same people to whom the man had previously been invisible.

I wonder how many **sexually confused young men** will grow up in our churches and no man will ever take them under their wing and teach them to be a man of God until one day when in confusion they declare themselves gay?

I wonder why it is that many a **young lady seeks desperate approval** by allowing men to misuse the body that God loaned her, as she cries out for love, and few seem to say a word until she is pregnant and alone.

We have a lot to say when someone sins. We can light up the phone-line then, but what about when their insecurities are displayed before… do we take the time? Do we even know their names?

People thought they knew what God wanted, but they had totally misjudged God's heart, because they were not truly sticking up for HIM, but trying to control THEM. The man wasn't told to break the Sabbath:

Genesis 1:1-2:3 offers the story of the seven days and the Sabbath. In 2:2-3 God stopped his creative labors, but He continued to maintain the life of the work He had built. Planets spun, solar systems turned. God wasn't creating anymore, but He wasn't completely passive either.

Later, in Exodus 20:8-11, God told the people not to work in a way that would add to their wealth and comfort.

What the people were referring to is specifically in Jeremiah 17:21ff. The people at the time of Jeremiah reasoned that they could carry burdens and make deliveries on the Sabbath as long as they weren't actually working. They were skirting intimacy with God and trying to pull a fast one on God. The first twenty verses of the chapter deal with the issue on the level of deceit, and that is exactly why God addressed it through Jeremiah. This man wasn't violating the Sabbath. He was removing an obstacle in order to make the path safe, and then heading to the Temple to worship and be declared clean! (5:13-14).

Only after the man encountered Jesus again was he aware of Who healed him, and ready to share that with others (5:15-16). All attention left the man as the leaders went after Jesus. The man became INVISIBLE AGAIN. Why? **They weren't asking him about the healing out of wonder or fascination – but out of a desire to CONTROL.**

It is deeply rooted in the heart of some people to run around controlling others. They believe that the ethical commands of the Bible are license to do just that.

Do not misunderstand me; I am not saying that all rules are bad things. I am saying that sharing God's ethical and moral standards was intended to be in the **deep desire to help the one that you are sharing with ("speaking the truth in love"** - Eph. 4:15, though there the original context appears to be believers who need instruction).

The **second attitude** that accompanies sharing of standards beyond a "love for the individual" is a **true and sustained intimacy with the Lord on the part of the one sharing.**

Apart from a walk with God and a singular desire to please Him daily, we become sounding gongs – dispensing unlived truths. This is often the heart of RELIGIOUS MEN—

attempting to control others they seem to care little about in practical life, and projecting a standard they are not truly living daily.

In contrast to these men, Jesus offers **seven lessons on PEOPLE OF FAITH** that must be noted, on our way to testing ourselves:

The Lessons: (John 5:17-47)

> **People of Faith understand the unique place of Jesus.** Jesus, Who is Lord of the Sabbath, claimed that He had the right to make the man work, since God ALWAYS WORKED on Sabbath (5:17-18). This was an overt claim not missed by those who heard it! They didn't try to make themselves equal to Him in understanding, nor had the right of judgment of others.

He knew the hearts of men, I don't. I CANNOT PRETEND TO TRULY KNOW THE MOTIVES of people, and I need to be careful not to act as though I do. Jesus is the eternal Son of God, I am an adopted son. I was born – He had conversation with His Father about coming to Earth prior to His arrival (Phil.2) and was the Agent of Creation (Col. 1:16-17; Heb. 1:3ff).

I do not possess His ability to know men, and I am not trying to get them to follow ME as He did – only to follow HIM as I DID.

> **People of Faith follow God's Word closely, and must always be careful not to equate that standard with GOD'S STANDARD** ("was breaking the Sabbath" refers to their idea, not God's idea!) (5:19).

> **People of Faith understand that direction comes through intimate connection with God.** Out of love **God showed Jesus what He wanted Him to accomplish**, and promised even greater demonstrations (5:20). This occurred as an example of how God worked with our Savior in sharing

truth. Truth comes through surrender of our lives to God, not simply to a standard we think He would like. Prayer is a key here. A great many Christians try to follow the Word without offering a word of their own to a Father Who does not hear from them. Where is the intimacy? Jesus spent time with the Father and taught His disciples to spend time with Him in prayer. **A relationship of following edicts is not intimate – it is sterile.**

People of Faith understand they cannot bypass what Jesus taught about life. We follow His Word and His example, while we grow in love through daily surrender. **We honor WHO HE IS by obedience to WHAT HE SAID.** He is the exalted Son of the Father. The **Son has the power of the Father** to give **life** (5:21) and to **judge** men and all things (5:22). The future will show this in the resurrection of the dead (5:25-30; cp. Revelation 20:11-15).

People of Faith long to be small, not big. They hunger to worship and exalt their God. The **Son will receive all the glory** that the Father has – an overt statement of worship (5:23; as with Thomas in John 20:28).

People of Faith are convinced there is only one path to walk upon. They aren't "Plan A" and "Plan B" spiritual walkers. They aren't "**many roads lead to Heaven**" kind of people. They understand the one and only **formula of eternal life** is this:

- Hear (Listen to and conform life to) My Word,
- Believe Father's sending (trust the source of My message as from the very Creator),
- Bypass judgment and
- LIVE **NOW**! (5:24).

People of Faith have three layers of foundation:

- The testimony of those that lead them to Christ:

People come to Christ because we share Him with our lives – something that only happens when we love and engage. That is what John did in John 1, He knew Jesus, and sent five men to follow after Him.

- The evidence of Jesus' work:

After the five men began to follow Jesus, they watched what He did in the lives of people around them. They watched His works, and felt His warmth. They marveled at His power and gazed at His greatness.

- The truth testimony of the Father shared through His Holy Word.

Finally they listened to His Words and tested them against the prophetic Word of the Living God.

Jesus offered **three witnesses:**

- My cousin (5:31-35);
- My works (5:36) and
- My Father and His disclosed Word (5:37-47).

Others were studying that same Word, but they were RELIGIOUS men, who studied the Word to gain control over other men. That isn't real faith, that's nothing but religion. They missed Him when He stood before them – not because He didn't fit the qualifications of Messiah, but because they COULD NOT CONTROL HIM.

Jesus called His followers to be people of FAITH not RELIGION. People of faith love lost people and want to walk daily and deeply with God.

Knowing Jesus
Lessons in the Gospel of John

Lesson Ten: John 6:1-71 "Eating is Believing - Six Principles of Real Fulfillment"

Mick Jagger brought the words to life: "I can't get no satisfaction!" He shouted it, but millions have felt it. They seek to find a way to fulfill the empty place in their hearts, and are sorely disappointed when fortune, fame, power, and pleasure let them down and leave them wanting.

Jesus offered six truths that fill the whole, because He made us and knows us. **The truth is - fulfillment starts with Him.** Jesus was a master teacher. He used a variety of settings to teach the disciples. John 6 offers a record of **two kinds of learning.** The **first** is found in two "**laboratory learning**" situations. Jesus put the disciples in learning situations that pointed out areas of weakness that each disciple needed to recognize and face change in. The first was on a hillside, where the disciples learned while serving crowds. The second lab was in the dark and on the sea – together, but without Jesus. The **second kind** of learning was "**lecture learning**" as Jesus taught first before the crowds and then intimately to His disciples.

Sandwiched in the lab settings were some critical lessons regarding COLLABORATION with Jesus. In the hillside lecture of Jesus, He explained fulfillment to the crowd, and then offered private keys to understanding to His close disciples.

Key Principle: Jesus is willing to share the secret of real and lasting fulfillment to those who will listen and take Him seriously.

"Hillside" Laboratory Test: Public Test for the Disciples (John 6:1-15)

The Set Up:

*John 6:1 After these things Jesus went away to the other side of the Sea of Galilee (or Tiberias). 2 A large crowd followed Him, because they saw the signs which He was performing on those who were sick. 3 Then Jesus went up on the mountain, and there He sat down with His disciples. 4 Now the Passover, the feast of the Jews, was near. 5 Therefore **Jesus**, lifting up His eyes and seeing that a large crowd was coming to Him, **said to Philip,** "**Where are WE to buy bread**, so that these may eat?" 6 This He was saying to test him, for He Himself knew what He was intending to do. 7 **Philip answered** Him, "**Two hundred denarii worth of bread is not sufficient** for them, for everyone to receive a little." 8 One of His disciples, **Andrew**, Simon Peter's brother, **said** to Him, 9 "**There is a lad here who has five barley loaves and two fish, but what are these for so many people?"***

- The **test** was to see if the disciples could grasp that with Jesus, every need could be met.
- Philip saw the limited resources (purse) of the **disciples** and concluded it was not possible.
- Andrew saw the limited resources (lunch box) of the **crowd** and concluded it was not possible.
- Neither disciple factored in **Jesus** nor how He could fulfill the needs.
- Jesus' question that set the test up included HIM, but it was easy for the disciples to set aside Jesus and not include Him.

Inclusion Principle: Jesus cooperates with us, but never leaves us to care for needs without Him. Without Him we can do nothing; through Him we can do all things. It was the tendency of the disciples to LEAVE HIM OUT; it was not His desire to be excluded.

The Example (6:10-15)

John 6:10 Jesus said, "Have the people sit down." Now there was much grass in the place. So the men sat down, in number about five thousand. 11 Jesus then took the loaves, and having given thanks, He distributed to those who were seated; likewise also of the fish as much as they wanted. 12 When they were filled, He said to His disciples, "Gather up the leftover fragments so that nothing will be lost." 13 So they gathered them up, and filled twelve baskets with fragments from the five barley loaves which were left over by those who had eaten. 14 Therefore when the people saw the sign which He had performed, they said, "This is truly the Prophet Who is to come into the world." 15 So Jesus, perceiving that they were intending to come and take Him by force to make Him king, withdrew again to the mountain by Himself alone.

- Jesus told the disciples to organize the people to receive from Him.
- Jesus took what the crowd gave to Him, and multiplied it to care for the need.
- Jesus gave sufficient to fill all that were gathered there.
- Jesus gave enough to care for the needs of the disciples
- Jesus taught His disciples through the reaction of the crowd in front of them – the problem provided the solution!

Obedience Principle: Jesus needs no plan on our part to do His work – only sufficient belief to produce obedience to His commands. When the disciples DID what He asked, He DID what only He could do!

"Boat in Darkness" Laboratory Test: Private Test for the Disciples (6:16-24)

*John 6:16 Now when evening came, His **disciples went down** to the sea, 17 and after getting into a boat, they* *started to cross the sea to Capernaum. It had already become **dark**, and Jesus had not yet come to them. 18 The **sea** began to be **stirred** up because a strong **wind** was **blowing**. 19 Then, when they had rowed about three or four miles, they saw Jesus walking on the sea and drawing near to the boat; and they were **frightened**. 20 But He said to them, "It is I; **do not** be afraid." 21 So they were willing to receive Him into the boat, and immediately the boat was at the land to which they were going. 22 The next day the crowd that stood on the other side of the sea saw that there was no other small boat there, except one, and that Jesus had not entered with His disciples into the boat, but that His disciples had gone away alone. 23 There came other small boats from Tiberias near to the place where they ate the bread after the Lord had given thanks. 24 So when the crowd saw that Jesus was not there, nor His disciples, they themselves got into the small boats, and came to Capernaum seeking Jesus.*

- The boat test was to underscore the hillside test – you cannot do this without Me. (Alone we are "down and dark" – 6:16-17).
- Troubles collide into our lives in the alone time (6:18).
- Any answer that we don't understand initially frightens us (we want what we can understand – 6:19).
- Jesus wants His presence to be enough to settle us (6:20).
- When we are prepared to receive Him, we will experience His power (6:21).
- People that don't see His power will not understand what changes us (6:22-24).

Request Principle: Jesus sees our troubles and both can and will work, but only when we see that we cannot do it without Him, and when we invite Him to work. "We have not because we ask not!"

Lecture One: Public Lesson before the Crowds (6:25-59)

6:25 When they found Him on the other side of the sea, they said to Him, "Rabbi, when did You get here?" 26 Jesus answered them and said, "Truly, truly, I say to you, you seek Me, not because you saw signs, but because you ate of the loaves and were filled. 27 Do not **work** for the food which perishes, but for the food which endures to eternal life, which the Son of Man will **give** to you, for on Him the Father, God, has set His seal."

Six Principles about Fulfillment:

Principle 1: Fulfillment is received and not attained. Only God can fill the hole in your heart, and He will only do so if you come on His terms.

John 6:28 Therefore they said to Him, "What shall we do, so that we may work the works of God?" 29 Jesus answered and said to them, "This is the work of God that you believe in Him whom He has sent."

Principle 2: Fulfillment comes from believing Me! Belief is the only thing that opens the door.

Hebrews 11:6 says: "And without faith it is impossible to please Him, for he who comes to God must believe that He is [i.e. exists in the form He claims to] and that He is a rewarder of those who seek Him"). John 6:47 repeats this idea.

*John 6:30 So they said to Him, "What then do You do for a sign, so that we may see, and believe You? What work do You perform? 31 Our fathers ate the manna in the wilderness; as it is written, 'HE GAVE THEM **BREAD** OUT OF HEAVEN **TO EAT**.'" 32 Jesus then said to them, "Truly, truly, I say to you, it is not Moses who has given you the bread out of Heaven, but it is My Father Who gives you the true bread out of Heaven. 33 For the bread of God is that which comes down out of*

*Heaven, and gives life to the world." 34 Then they said to Him, "Lord, always give us this bread." 35 Jesus said to them, "I am the **bread of life**; he who comes to Me will not hunger, and he who believes in Me will never thirst. 36 But I said to you that you have seen Me, and yet do not believe. 37 All that the Father gives Me will come to Me, and the one who comes to Me I will certainly not cast out. 38 For I have come down from Heaven, not to do My own will, but the will of Him Who sent Me. 39 This is the will of Him Who sent Me, that of all that He has given Me I lose nothing, but raise it up on the last day."*

Principle 3: Fulfillment that comes from the Father is in a different form than ever before! (and possibly a different form than you are looking for!) Note that the people "missed the point" of Jesus' coming (they wanted more physical bread for now, not commitment to Him for the future!)

In 2003, a popular Christian professor and an aide wrote a book as a critique of contemporary American Christianity. The title was **Adventures In Missing The Point!** The book is an examination of how the church in modern America is living out the Christian faith in this new millennium. The question concerns whether modern disciples are "getting it."

There are still people who are **only interested in the loaves and the fishes**. Christian missionaries in 19th-century India used to describe those who came to the mission stations simply for food as "rice Christians" - so long you give them free rice, they'll be back.

Today, across America some churches are finding that new people are coming in. Things are exciting! We're getting lively **music**, neat sound **equipment**, cool **spotlights**, quality **dramas**, need-oriented **preaching**, and magnificent **musicals**. Morale is **up**. Attendance is **up**. Excitement is **up**! **But is godliness up? Commitment?**

Jack Hayford said at one point not long ago, "They come for the show, but refuse to grow." One such pastor lamented: "Our people are converted in every way except their **mind-set**, **lifestyle**, and **values**."

Exactly. We must be careful now. We are often willing to listen as long as what they hear is **positive**, **helpful**, and non-offensive - like talk about sin and repentance or any of that negative or painful stuff. We will be a shallow bunch but a happy lot signing up for classes on CPR or 'How to make your child mind without losing yours.' But when it comes to committed discipleship, no thanks, they will pass. **If we are not careful we too can be guilty of wanting what Christ gives and not Christ Himself. We will effectively miss the point.**

John 6:40 For this is the will of My Father, that everyone who beholds the Son and believes in Him will have eternal life, and I Myself will raise him up on the last day.

> **Principle 4: Fulfillment is accepting Me now, for a future blessing!**

*John 6:41 Therefore the Jews were grumbling about Him, because He said, "I am the bread that came down out of Heaven." 42 They were saying, "Is not this Jesus, the son of Joseph, Whose father and mother we know? How does He now say, 'I have come down out of Heaven'?" 43 Jesus answered and said to them, "Do not grumble among yourselves. 44 No one can come to Me unless the Father Who sent Me **draws** him; and I will raise him up on the last day. 45 It is written in the prophets, 'AND THEY SHALL ALL BE TAUGHT OF GOD.' Everyone who has **heard** and **learned** from the Father comes to Me."*

> **Principle 5: Fulfillment comes to those who obey the drawing call of the Father!**

*John 6:46 "Not that anyone has seen the Father, except the One who is from God; He has seen the Father. 47 Truly, truly, I say to you, he who believes has eternal life. 48 I am the bread of life. 49 Your fathers ate the manna in the wilderness, and they **died**. 50 This is the bread which comes down out of Heaven, so that one may eat of it and **not die**. 51 I am the living bread that came down out of Heaven; if anyone eats of this bread, he will live forever; and the bread also which I will give for the life of the world is My flesh." 52 Then the Jews began to argue with one another, saying, "How can this man give us His flesh to eat?" 53 So Jesus said to them, "Truly, truly, I say to you, **unless you eat the flesh of the Son of Man and drink His blood, you have no life in yourselves.** 54 He who eats My flesh and drinks My blood has eternal life, and I will raise him up on the last day. 55 For My flesh is true food, and My blood is true drink. 56 He who eats My flesh and drinks My blood abides in Me, and I in him. 57 As the living Father sent Me, and I live because of the Father, so **he who eats Me, he also will live** because of Me. 58 This is the bread which came down out of Heaven; not as the fathers ate and died; he who eats this bread will live forever." 59 These things He said in the synagogue as He taught in Capernaum.*

Principle 6: Your permanent fulfillment comes at a price I will pay for you! The picture of intimacy and transformation from within was graphically offered, but not easily understood.

Here is where the title comes from – "Eating is Believing" because that is His point.

Lecture Two: Private Lesson to the Disciples (6:60-65)

John 6:60 Therefore many of His disciples, when they heard this said, "This is a difficult statement; who can listen to it?" 61 But Jesus, conscious that His disciples grumbled at this, said to them, "Does this cause you to stumble? 62 What then if you see the Son of Man ascending to where He was before? 63 It is the Spirit Who gives life; the flesh profits nothing; the words that I have spoken to you are spirit and are life. 64 But there are some of you who do not believe." For Jesus knew from the beginning who they were who did not believe, and who it was that would betray Him. 65 And He was saying, "For this reason I have said to you, that no one can come to Me unless it has been granted him from the Father."

Four Keys to Fulfillment:

- Disciples must see Jesus in His place – **Who** is Jesus?
- Disciples must understand where real life is – **Where** does Jesus fulfill us?
- Disciples must understand that only believers will get it – **What** does Jesus require of us?
- Disciples must understand that God enables the process. **How** does a believer find the truth?

Reality Principle: Until we understand the place of Jesus, and recognize that reality is primarily in the spiritual realm (the physical is a reflection) we are not prepared to believe. When those truths are accepted and we change our lives to conform to the truth, God opens new doors to us.

Three Responses to Jesus: (6:66-71)

John 6:66 As a result of this many of His disciples withdrew and were not walking with Him anymore. 67 So Jesus said to the twelve, "You do not want to go away also, do you?" 68 Simon Peter answered Him, "Lord, to whom shall we go? You have words of eternal life. 69 We have believed and have come to know that You are the Holy One of God." 70 Jesus answered them, "Did I Myself not choose you, the twelve, and yet one of you is a devil?" 71 Now He meant Judas the son of Simon Iscariot, for he, one of the twelve, was going to betray Him.

- Some **left** to seek fulfillment elsewhere (6:66).
- Some **remained** and **understood** He had the truth (6:67-69).
- Some **stayed** but weren't **real** (6:70)

"Tares" Principle: Not all that leave are lost forever (some will return). Not all that stay are truly "with the program" – as in the wheat and tares story.

Jesus holds the key to real and lasting fulfillment. He has always been willing to share the secret to those who would listen and take Him seriously.

Knowing Jesus
Lessons in the Gospel of John

Lesson 11: John 7:1-53 "Six Places the Truth Cannot Be Found!"

Both Johnny Lee and Waylon Jennings popularized the song "Looking for love in all the wrong places" and many of us can sympathize in our personal histories with having done just that. We sought someone that would be right for us, and found many along the journey that, well... weren't. Still others today tell a similar tale about discovering the TRUTH found in Jesus. We looked at a lot of other places, but found out – you can't find the right answer **when looking in the wrong place**.

Key Principle: The truth about Jesus is found in a personal encounter with Him and His claims, not in the wisdom of this world.

The Truth Search will be successful:

Not by POP re-framing of Jesus but <u>choosing to face the true Jesus</u> (John 7:1-13)

Jesus didn't want to openly walk in Judea because of death threats (7:1). Even though He had the power, He didn't purposely test the enemy's powers to arrest or organize a pre-emptive move. Jesus used His mind, not just His ability.

A feast arose in which He was to be obedient to the Word and attend, exposing Him to danger (7:2). He went because obedience was not an option when it came to the Word!

Now to the heart of the issue: POPULARITY. His brothers wanted Him to go with them "that Your disciples also may see Your works which you are doing" (7:3). They wanted Him to "show Yourself to the world" (7:4). Yet, Jesus knew this **didn't come from believing hearts**, but by hearts motivated by something else (7:5).

Pastor Jerry Shirley rightly noted: The World's Most Popular Religion is a RELIGION THAT DOES NOT INSIST. It will not insist on . . . **Repentance:** Remember, Jesus said, "Except ye repent, ye shall all likewise perish." **Regeneration:** Though the Bible insists that, "Ye must be born again." **Restitution:** We don't want to be forced to live through the pain of straightening out those things we've done that can be made right again. **Retribution:** We cannot insist on retribution and eternal Hell at the end of a sinful life. Only the positive, no judgment. A lot of people will come as long as there is no "insistence" in your religion... The World's Most Popular Religion is a RELIGION THAT DOES NOT INTERFERE.. Popular religion does not interfere with pleasures, customs, hobbies, habits, jobs, families and personal plans. If you can come up with a religion that will let man be, do, and go when and where he wants to, without having any interference, it will be popular. In other words, most people want a religious coat that they can put on when they go to church and take off and hang in the closet when they get home! You hear in the church: "I'd rather have a Sat. night service or an early morning service so I can keep my Sunday free." Funny, it used to be called "the Lord's Day" in our culture until the NFL got it! We have come to own all our time and be gods ourselves and answerable to no one... "I'm right, you're wrong, and even if you force me to do something, I'll still go away knowing I'm in charge!" That's rebellion! Even Christians have authority problems and hold back God's blessings when they won't be led, won't follow, and always feel they know better.

Proverbs 29:1 A man who hardens his neck after much reproof will suddenly be broken beyond remedy.

Some want to follow the POP Jesus. The one that gets them elected because of endorsing Him means getting votes from unsuspecting voters. Others want to be with the POP Jesus that says kind things and loves everybody. Some want the POP Jesus of Christmas that gives us days off, warm and fuzzy feelings of yesteryear, and traditions of family, hearth and home. They want the baby Jesus, meek and mild. They want the gentle Jesus that offers a message to lambs and babies and children. The problem is the POP Jesus isn't the TRUE Jesus. The true Jesus has a message that men are sinners in need of salvation. The true Jesus has a message that we can't find God through well cherished practices of our own making and choosing. The true Jesus says that we have to admit our own bankruptcy of Spirit and cling to nothing that is good in ourselves. The true Jesus stomps out our pride and doesn't let us have our toys and fantasies that aren't pleasing to Him. The true Jesus demands humility before Him, obedience to Him, and glory for Him. **He isn't the POP Jesus at all!**

That is why Jesus told them that they could go without Him (7:6), because they were in no danger from the world as they offered no message that offended the world (7:7). His issue wasn't **DEATH** (which He knew would eventually take place) but **TIMING** (7:8).

He remained behind, and followed later silently as people sought to find Him (7:10-13).

The unbelieving world (even if they seem as close as a "brother") cannot offer Jesus to anyone. They boil down and re-distill His teachings into some benign "do good" toothless philosophy. They repackage and resell the "talking points" that match the Jesus they want to know. The problem is: Truth is found by looking in the right place. **The right place isn't the "handlers" and "pop experts" but facing what He really did, hearing what He really said.**

    Not by adding Jesus to our agenda but <u>surrendering to His Father's purposes</u> (7:14-18)

Jesus arrived at the feast and showed up teaching inside the Temple (7:14). The Judean leaders didn't question the SUBSTANCE of His message, but the ORIGIN of it (7:15). Jesus didn't have a pedigree or diploma from one of their organizations – but He did possess a compelling message and a following. They were puzzled because they assumed if someone was going to be 'right' he would come from their pre-defined circle.

John 7:16 So Jesus answered them and said, "My teaching is not Mine, but His Who sent Me. 17 If anyone is willing to do His will, he will know of the teaching whether it is of God or whether I speak from Myself. 18 He who speaks from himself seeks his own glory; but He Who is seeking the glory of the One Who sent Him, He is true and there is no unrighteousness in Him."

The issue wasn't that they couldn't see the truth of what Jesus was teaching the people. The problem was that **He wasn't leading the people toward THEM and THEIR ORGANIZATION**, but to exalt God without them. **They wanted to be in the picture. They were the authorities**. They wanted the power to hold the door open or close it. If they could surrender the power hunger and willingly cling to God's mercy and desire His glory, they could hear the message that Jesus brought.

You cannot get the truth by trying to add it to the other preconceived notions of your life. They must be surrendered. Jesus' truth will not **ring** in your heart while you **cling** to your sinful practices and indulge your lustful passions. He will not share His truth with you while you use His reputation simply to build your business, to make life about your comfort and about your wishes. **He will reign only in a heart that surrenders to the Father's glory,** and the Father's reign. He will not visit part time, and require only partial surrender. He is not interested in furthering your goals ("Your best life now" is not his real goal!) –

He desires that you further the goals of His Father in Heaven. All the personal benefits are side issues, not the motivation.

I believe the Lord recorded this because He knows that we miss the obvious!

There was a man named Pedro who lived near the Mexican border. One day Pedro walked up to the border station with a wheelbarrow full of sand. The border guard suspected Pedro was trying to smuggle something illegal into the country so he carefully sifted through the sand. When he didn't find anything, he let Pedro pass. The next day Pedro showed up at the border with another wheelbarrow full of sand. This time the border guard made Pedro empty the sand out of the wheelbarrow and then he sifted through it. He turned the wheelbarrow over, inspected every inch of it but found nothing so he let Pedro pass again. This went on day in and day out for three years straight. The guard said to Pedro, "I know what you're thinking Pedro, you think that you will wear me down and one day I won't check the wheelbarrow and then you'll sneak something in. Well that's not going to happen. I'm going to keep on checking you every time you come through here and one day I'll catch you and then it will be over for you. One day Pedro stopped coming. Several months later the border guard was in Mexico and saw Pedro getting out of a brand new car dressed in a beautifully tailored suit. The border guard ran up to Pedro and asked him how it came to be that he was doing so well. Pedro said, "While you were searching through the sand for illegal contraband, I brought 1825 brand new wheelbarrows into the country and sold them at a handsome profit!"

We can't see the obvious much of the time, so Jesus made sure the people understood that following His Father was about surrendering themselves to HIS POWER, not trying to add Him to THEIR AGENDA!

Not by surface impressions but by <u>understanding God's purposes</u> (7:19-24)

The men before Jesus desired to see Him eliminated and Jesus not only called them on it, but told them it violated the ethics of the Law (7:19). The people who didn't know the plots thought He lost control of His mind to a paranoid demon (7:20) because they saw the beauty of the Temple, observed the flowing robes of the leaders, and smelled the smoke of the Temple sacrifice. They judged truth based on the appearance of holy things and powerful and prestigious symbols. **They didn't know the truth, because the truth isn't always obvious.** The discussion between two people may have a level that goes well beyond what you can see and hear.

Jesus answered them: "You all marvel when I do something spectacular, but the leaders come after me for a healing on the Sabbath that is no different than keeping the Law and circumcising a baby on the Sabbath. Don't judge based on what you see, the truth is more complicated than the outward appearance." (R. Smith paraphrase)

Some people think the most prestigious church is the right church. They judge truth on a "might makes right" mentality. If the **crowds** are bigger, the message is **truer** or better. If the **offerings** are **larger** the blessing shows **God's hand** is there. **Has that proven true? Haven't televangelists churned out huge sums of money while visiting prostitutes and making back-room deals for more selfishness?**

Wouldn't a better judgment be made if we took the time to observe what the **core message** offered was, or how they **USED** the money that was set in their hands by sacrificial givers? Is the truth found by who appears to GET more, or who appears to USE WISELY the monies given for **KINGDOM PURPOSES?** Is the truth found by which rally is larger, or by which one had an argument that squares with the exposed purposes of God's heart?

Jesus called the people back to the Sabbath healing and showed it was consistent with the **PURPOSE** of God, and not contradictory. In clear words, He argued that the priest and Levites may have the **POWER AND PRESTIGE**, but they did not have the right IDEA because they didn't have the right understanding of God's PURPOSES.

Not by man-made traditions but by real intimacy with God (7:25-29)

The people were confused by hearing that Jesus was marked by some leaders for death, and yet suspecting that Jesus may have been the promised Anointed One (7:25-26). It seemed unthinkable that a man could present such a simple and believable exposition of God's heart and be insane. At the same time, He was getting away with saying some very tough things in their Temple. How could this be? Maybe He was right, and things weren't as they appeared. People wondered.

What squelched the question was a **commonly held tradition** that Messiah would not come from a known place (7:27). Because they had such a tradition, and assumed it to be true, they missed the Truth – when He stood right in front of them.

How often our preconceived notions and commonly held ideas trump truth. We THINK we know something, so we turn down any explanation that doesn't fit that "KNOWLEDGE" even though it may be the very thing we need to consider.

Jesus didn't dispute the tradition, because that was pointless. They weren't going to be changed by His attack on what they believed, but by His call to replace that belief with something that was the truth. In other words, Jesus went about trying to get them to focus on their real need – a living and intimate walk with His Father that they did not possess (7:28-29).

In the absence of a real faith, a real religion is always the next best fit. The problem is that religion is empty in the inner recesses of the heart where doubt creeps in. Relationship with God fills the holes that religion (a set of practices in hope to please or appease God) cannot reach.

Why are people hooked to traditions that aren't in the Word? Because life is constantly changing, and it makes us feel better to be attached to the past.

There have been more changes in the last 50 years than there has ever been before in history all put together. More information has been recorded in the last thirty years than in the previous five thousand years. More than one-half the scientists who have ever lived are alive today. Ninety percent of all the items in the supermarket today did not exist just ten years ago. It is estimated that 73% of college graduates are going into jobs which did not exist when they were born – 22 short years ago.

I am highlighting the changes we have all seen just in our lifetimes. Sometimes it seems that life is going by so fast it confuses us and all we want to do is hibernate away from the changes where it is more comfortable and we don't have to be bothered with thinking about it. But we cannot afford to hide our heads in the sand. To do so would not gain us anything worthwhile. We must know what is around us at all times. Everything we're familiar with is changing, right before our eyes. We are forever on the move – if you can name it, we humans are doing it! The pace is somewhere between maddening and insane.

And in all that people want to be connected to something from the past... something, well... traditional. That isn't

wrong, but the strong pull can blind us that things we feel strongly about may not be true at all. We need to be careful.

Religiously, sometimes we hold to certain practices more because of our love for those who taught us those things than for the truths themselves.

    Not by performances but by receiving the Spirit of God (7:30-39)

The leaders sought to get Jesus but the crowds seemed to be listening more intently (7:30-31a). Yet, another hindrance came into their acceptance of the truth. They thought the coming of Messiah was certainly to be filled with open manifestations and miracles. It is not such a strange expectation, is it? (7:31b). Even today I hear people ask, "If God wants people to follow Him, why doesn't He do more spectacular things that will make it obvious that He is there?" It sounds reasonable until you look into a telescope or a microscope and listen to the alternative explanations of the origins of man: a big bang, a cosmic fluke from nothingness through amoeba, fish, money and man. It doesn't seem like man has problems following mythology that places no expectation on his moral development. **He is always ready for a philosophy that answers his longing by allowing him to act to suit his own lusts at any moment.**

Sensing that the crowd would not stop them from taking Him into questioning, some Pharisees attempted to find the right time and place for his apprehension (7:32).

Jesus answered their attempts with two promises. The first was that there would come a day when the time would be right for His departure to a place they could not reach (7:33-36). The people weren't sure where the journey would take Jesus (possibly the Diaspora?), but Jesus did not clarify. His purpose was to tell them that the timing of His work was already preset, and that even Temple leadership was not going to change it.

They would not reach Him until He was ready and the Father delivered Him into their hands.

This is a theme throughout the book – Jesus was obedient to His Father's timetable, and it would not be interrupted. He protected that time. He didn't deliberately expose Himself to any possible violation of it. He would travel quietly when they wanted to get Him until the Father said otherwise.

His second promise was for their immediate attention. He waited on the WATER LIBATION ceremony of the last day of Sukkot. The women came up from the pool of Siloam carrying their water pitchers. The ceremony occurred every day of the feast, but on the last day they brought not a full jug of water, but an empty one. They were seeking God for the water of life that came from above – they were praying for rains. Jesus waited for that day (7:37) and called out to the crowd, "I am the source of the water that you really need. If you are thirsty, I can offer you the way to water that will flow from inside out!" He was making a promise of the Spirit to come, but said that it could come only to those who were prepared to get it by invitation of the Son (7:38-39).

The people wanted miracles on the outside, but Jesus offered power to come from Heaven and flow through them. His condition was that they receive it through receiving Him. They needed to believe, or they got nothing. The empowering of God's Spirit, later marked by outer manifestations, was not to replace Jesus, but to point to Jesus. Accepting Him was the prerequisite to getting empowered. People wanted outward power to placate their curiosity and care for their physical needs – Jesus offered a power source that would flow through a relationship with Him into their hearts and then manifest itself by an outflow from their hearts to the lost world around them.

Finding the truth isn't just a **response** to the **external**, it requires the deep **surrender** of the **internal**. It is the surrender to Jesus and His message, and the surrender to the constant inner inspection of the Spirit. **It is the conscious surrender from privacy to the shared life of walking in the Spirit who lives WITHIN us**.

Not by closed-hearted experts but by <u>true searching</u> (7:40-53)

Some people expressed that Jesus was a prophet (7:40) others thought He was the Messiah (7:41a), while still others kept tripping over their ideas about what the Messiah would be (7:41b-42). The crowd was divided (7:43) with some wanting Him seized and questioned further. Even those sent to apprehend him couldn't seem to follow directions and grab Him, because it seemed wrong to them (7:45-46). The men who actually encountered Jesus couldn't dismiss Him. They said, "No one has spoken like Him" (7:46). They weren't ready to simply lump Him into the long list of self-promoting wind bags. That wasn't Jesus! He was unique and they knew it. They listened and could tell this wasn't fluff, it was more.

The legal minds were prepared to judge the man sight unseen. Without careful examination, they knew that **He wasn't ONE OF THEM** and that was all they needed to really know. They acted as though bringing Him in for questions would clarify their positions, but they had their minds made up already. Even an open-minded Pharisee could see that (7:47-53).

They didn't want to QUESTION Him to learn anything. They wanted to EXPOSE Him because they were already sure.

IF THEY WERE TO TAKE JESUS SERIOUSLY, THEY WOULD NEED TO SUBMIT TO HIM, AND THAT WASN'T GOING TO HAPPEN!

Error is multiform; truth is one. A thousand lies will live together, and tolerate each other. A thousand false gods will stand together; but if the ark of the true God enters Dagon's temple, Dagon must come down on his face and be dashed to pieces. Jehovah is God alone, and will not accept a rival. Truth is of necessity intolerant of error. Holiness cannot endure sin, righteousness cannot bear injustice, and truth cannot consort with error. "What concord hath Christ with Belial?"

How like that are many people today! When Jesus is presented to them, **what they know about Christianity or history discounts their desire to even hear His words**. They have their mind made up, and that is all there is to it. Jesus doesn't qualify because they are already sure it is a **HOAX**.

Yet is that the real problem? **Look more closely at the men that were "experts" and what they were protecting was their POWER and CONTROL.**

That is the real issue and it has always been the issue. This isn't just a problem for ancient Pharisees, it is a modern problem for those who hear the message of Jesus. **They want what JESUS BRINGS but not at the expense of LOSING CONTROL of all that they perceive to grasp**. They don't want a Jesus that questions their thought life, or a Jesus that reaches into their wallet and reorients their priorities. They want a Jesus Who is an absent-minded prophet that will allow them to have **WHAT HE GIVES** without inviting inside **WHO HE IS**. The sad part is, they don't really listen to Him and discover the beauty of surrendering to Him.

The truth about Jesus isn't found in the wisdom of this world, but in a personal encounter with Him and His claims.

Knowing Jesus
Lessons in the Gospel of John

Lesson Twelve: John 8:1-20 "The 'Do Over' Grace of God"

"I wasn't ready!" the boy replied when the first ball flew across the plate. "That's a 'do over' throw," he called. There was some grumbling, but usually he was a decent batter, so we figured he was telling the truth. Ah, the old days of neighborhood wiffle ball games in the summer. I love do-overs if they are FOR ME.

We don't always get them, and we can't presume on them, but it is just like our Father to offer second chances -- even when we KNOW we don't deserve them!

Key Principle: A personal relationship with the God of grace will set you free from shame! Walking in darkness and without a focus on relationship will leave you in shame.

In Max Lucado's book, *He Still Moves Stones,* he writes of this incident we find in John 8:1-11, and says: Rebecca Thompson fell twice from Fremont Canyon Bridge. She died both times. The first fall broke her heart; the second broke her neck. She was only eighteen years of age when she and her 11 year old sister were abducted by a pair of hoodlums near a store in Casper, Wyoming. They drove the girls forty miles southwest to the Fremont Canyon Bridge, a one-lane, steel beamed structure rising 112 feet above the North Platte River. The men brutally beat and raped Rebecca. She somehow convinced them not to do the same to her sister Amy. Both were thrown over the bridge into the narrow gorge. Amy died when she landed on a rock near the river but Rebecca slammed into a ledge and was ricocheted into deeper water. With a hip fractured in five places, she struggled to the shore. To protect her body from the cold, she wedged herself between two rocks and waited until the dawn. But the dawn never came for Rebecca. Oh, the sun came up and she was found. The physicians treated her wounds, and the courts imprisoned her attackers.

Life continued, but the dawn never came. So in September 1992, 19 years later, she returned to the bridge. Against her boyfriend's pleadings, she drove 70 mph to the North Platte River. With her two year old daughter and boyfriend at her side, she sat on the edge of the Fremont Canyon Bridge and wept. Through her tears she retold the story. The boyfriend didn't want the child to see her mother cry, so he carried the toddler to the car. That's when he heard the body hit the water. And that's when Rebecca Thompson died her second death. But why...was it fear? She had testified against the men, pointing them out in the courtroom. One of them taunted her by smirking and sliding his finger across his throat. The day she died the two murderers were up for parole. Was it guilt? Some think so. Despite Rebecca's attractive smile and appealing personality, friends say that she struggled with the ugly fact that she survived and her little sister had not. Was it shame? Everyone she knew and thousands she didn't had heard the humiliating details of her tragedy. She had been raped. She had been violated. She had been shamed.

Canyons of shame run deep, gorges of never-ending guilt, walls ribboned with the greens and grays of death, unending echoes of screams. Put your hands over your ears. Splash water on your face. Stop looking over your shoulder. Try as you might to outrun yesterday's tragedies, their tentacles are longer than your hope. They draw you back to the bridge of sorrows to be shamed again and again and again. Sometimes your shame is private, pushed over the edge by an abusive spouse, molested by a perverted parent, seduced by a compromising superior. No one else knows. But you know. And that's enough. Sometimes your shame is public, branded by a divorce you didn't want, contaminated by a disease you never expected, marked by a handicap you didn't create. And whether it's in your imagination or in the reality of others you're marked. Labeled: a divorcee, an invalid, an orphan, an AIDS patient. ...

And there are many Rebecca Thompsons in the Bible. So many in fact, that it almost seems that the pages of Scripture are stitched together with their stories. But there is one woman whose story embodies them all. A story of failure. A story of abuse. A story of shame. A story of grace... (*Sermon Central Illustrations*)

The Setting: An Autumn morning on the Temple porch during Sukkot (8:1-2)

After a day of confrontation with Judean leadership, the crowds went home, but Jesus went to the Mount of Olives. He may have been camping or lodging there, or He may have made His way to Bethany by way of the mountain ascent to the east of the city. It seems likely that He stayed nearby, because early the next morning He came back to the Temple, sat down and began teaching a growing gathering of people (7:53-8:2).

Three Problems in Obscuring Facts to Get "Truth" (8:3-9):

Scribes and Pharisees brought a woman into the porch area outside the Temple's holy precincts where they were going to convict her of adultery, and then take her outside of the city for stoning. (8:3-4). They saw Jesus teaching and used the opportunity to bring Him under condemnation as well (8:6) by asking Him, "Teacher, this woman was 'caught in the act' in adultery (clearly and without question in violation of the Law 8:4). Because the Law commands her death, what should we do?" (8:5).

Religious people often aren't asking what they sound like they are asking. Religion is about **control** – about being right and making others right. That's why I don't want to be religious. I want a relationship with God to control my life, and I want that same relationship to control yours – not ME, not THE CHURCH... your CREATOR and YOU. I want a GRACE life...

You are no doubt familiar with the cartoon characters Calvin and Hobbes, aren't you? Well they are walking along in the cartoon strip and Calvin says, "You know what the problem is with the universe?" Waiting for the shoe to drop, Hobbes responds, "What?" Calvin answers, "There's no toll-free customer service hot line for complaints! That's why things don't get fixed. If the universe had any decent management, we'd get a full refund if we weren't completely satisfied!" Hobbes objects: "But hey, the universe is free." To which Calvin retorts: "See, that's another thing. They should have a cover charge and keep out all the riffraff."

If we're honest, many of us wish that the riffraff would just go away or that they be punished. We tend to be pretty tough on people when they do things that bother us. We clamor for God's justice to be poured out on others, while we ourselves long for God's grace.

Problem One: The wrong people will not do the right thing, the right way, for the right reason.

These were tests by men who did not want to know God, nor walk in truth. They wanted control. They wanted power. They wanted people to fear them and follow them. There were two tests being played out by the Judean leaders – one in the life of the woman, and one in the life of Jesus. Though they were testing others, in the end it was the **leaders** that failed!

Isaiah 5:20 reminds us that much of what is wrong is inside. Woe unto them that call evil good, and good evil; that put darkness for light, and light for darkness; that put bitter for sweet, and sweet for bitter!

At that moment, Jesus did not respond, but stooped and wrote something in the dirt (ironic that he was drawing in the dirt while they were trying to kick up dust, isn't it? 8:6b). Sensing they may have Him trapped, they moved in for the kill. "What then do you say?" they persisted. He stood to address the men and said, "He who is without sin among you, let him be the first to throw a stone at her." (cp. Dt. 17:7; 8:7). He stooped again, intent to continue His dirt script. (8:8).

Problem Two: You cannot change reality by twisting the rules!

They knew who should raise the offense. This offense had a lawful injured party, but HE wasn't speaking, because HE also had guilt. There is more to the story than what the story appeared to be. That is the problem with people who seek personal control and not passionate relationship with God – they end up proving what they believe and believing what they prove – even when it isn't the truth.

People are not caught in the **act of adultery by themselves**.

Lev. 20: 10 If there is a man who commits adultery with another man' wife, one who commits adultery with his friend's wife, the adulterer and the adulteress shall surely be put to death

Where's the **man**? Why are the Pharisees only interested in humiliating this woman? **The stone throwing began before anyone ever picked up a rock (as is often the case!).** It began with a **malicious intent to discredit Jesus** no matter who got harmed in the process.

Add to that the fact that Deuteronomy 17:7 offers the woman's husband the right to cast the first stone. He was the **wounded** party. **If he was innocent** of adultery, than he could pick up the stone. If he wasn't, he had better drop the rock before the whole story came out. There are often two sides to these stories.

Hearing the lawful terms, the men knew the offended party was not innocent, **nor were they** for overlooking his sin to do what they were choosing. With no accuser to throw a stone, they dissipated into the crowd and side chambers – the oldest and most experienced first, leaving the woman without the crowd of accusers (8:9).

Problem Three: You cannot control the story once the facts are obvious.

When you are lying, making the truth look silly will backfire! The men made their play and Jesus answered their nonsense with truth. Without an accuser, the process broke down, as it was intended in the Law to do. Jesus wasn't arguing that the woman was innocent. He didn't ask them how they knew she was guilty. It was enough for Him that they said so, and He knew that part of the story was true. Yet, He was doing nothing wrong when they sought to trap Him. It simply left them without credibility and embarrassed.

The Example: Grace and Truth to the Disgraced (8:10-11)

With those He was teaching still eying the situation, Jesus stood, faced the woman and asked, "Woman, where are they? Did no one condemn you?" 11 She said, "No one, Lord." And Jesus said, "I do not condemn you, either. Go. From now on sin no more."

In John 1:17 we learned that **grace and truth came through Jesus**. Here is a good example of it. The truth is that **everyone in this story walked away with a second chance**. The Pharisees walked away with a chance to think twice about how they should respond to Jesus Christ. The crowd walked away with a chance to think about their own need for grace and realize their own need for forgiveness. The woman walked away with a chance to leave her life of sin, a chance to be made whole by the grace of God, a chance to end her adulterous lifestyle and to come back to the God of second chances.

The only One who can condemn doesn't. The One Who has the power to pass judgment, states the truth – then acquits. The One Who can point the finger refuses. Jesus wasn't as interested in picking up a rock as lighting a candle and making the truth set the woman free!

The Teaching: Grasping the Grace of the "God of Second Chances" changes us! (8:12-20)

(If the discussion was in the same setting, Jesus moved away from the woman to the Treasury area on the side of the Court of the Women, where the Menorah remained alight throughout this feast - cp. 8:20). Jesus turned to the crowd and offered **three lessons** about encountering the "God of Second Chances":

First, He said, *"I am the Light of the world. He who follows Me will not walk in the darkness, but will have the Light of life." (8:12).*

Lesson One: Knowing the "God of Second Chances" makes us willing to leave the security of the dark!

There is darkness and there is light. This world is filled with people that obscure the truth and try to live in the shadows, hiding their real intentions from everyone – even sometimes themselves. Those who walk with Jesus get out of that trap and walk in the truth. They seek to see things as they are, beginning in themselves, and then in their relationships. They realize the dark world is all about them. They simply will not be content to live in the shadows anymore. They hunger for the truth, no matter what it causes them to see in themselves – because they have in Jesus someone Who will love them through their old stains and darkness and allow them to change. He is the Grace-giver – the God of second chances.

Some Pharisees still observing Him raised an issue of legal etiquette: *"You are testifying about Yourself; Your testimony is not true"* (they applied a technical argument about testifying before the leadership in common speech, because they considered His speech to be "before them" - or for their benefit). *Jesus, Who was not merely impressing them had no such restriction. He replied: Even if I testify about Myself, My testimony is true, for I know where I came from and where I am going (8:13-14).*

Lesson Two: Knowing the "God of Second Chances" opens us to leaving the games we play with the truth for a simpler life!

When we walk in the dark world without a heart relationship to our Creator through His Son, we are disconnected from origin, purpose, and destiny. We open ourselves to the blame game of the Garden of Eden, the guilt and shame of a life cut off from its purpose. In the absence of relationship, we have only the LAWS and RULES of that God, and we feel judged and condemned by them – so we either keep our distance or create a set of religious control principles that enable us to live at peace with ourselves. Only when we know the God Who created us, and are secure in His love, are we willing and able to release the games we play for truth about ourselves, and about the world around us.

8:15-20 Jesus continued, 15 You judge according to the flesh; I am not judging anyone. 16 But even if I do judge, My judgment is true; for I am not alone in it, but I and the Father who sent Me. 17 Even in your law it has been written that the testimony of two men is true. 18 I am He who testifies about Myself, and the Father who sent Me testifies about Me." 19 So they were saying to Him, "Where is Your Father?" Jesus answered, "You know neither Me nor My Father; if you knew Me, you would know My Father also." 20 These words He spoke in the treasury, as He taught in the temple; and no one seized Him, because His hour had not yet come.

Lesson Three: Knowing the "God of Second Chances" enables me to make judgments with His heart and purpose at the forefront!

In my dark life away from God, I had only the darkness to give me the feeling of safety. Now in the light and relationship with God, I can see things more clearly and increasingly (as I grow in Him) through standards that are consistent with both a Holy and Gracious God. In practical terms, the closer I get to Him through listening to His Word and surrendering to His Spirit, the more I think like Him. The more I think like Him, the more life makes sense and my standards are consistent and pleasing to Him.

A few years ago a book came out called, ***I Kissed Dating Goodbye,*** by Joshua Harris. "In 'The Room'... There were not distinguishing features of the room except for one wall covered with small index-card files. They were like the ones in libraries that list titles by author or subject in alphabetical order. But these files, which stretched from floor to ceiling... had very different headings... The first to catch my attention was one that read, "Girls I Have Liked." And then without being told, I knew exactly where I was. This lifeless room with its small files was a crude catalog system for my life. Here were written the actions of every moment, big and small, in a detail my memory couldn't match.

"A sense of wonder and curiosity, coupled with horror, stirred within me as I began randomly opening files and exploring their contents. Some brought joy and sweet memories; others a sense of shame and regret so intense that I would look over my shoulder to see if anyone was watching me. A file named "Friends" was next to one marked "Friends I Have Betrayed." The titles ranged from the mundane to the outright weird. "Books I Have Read." "Jokes I've Laughed At." "Things I've Done in Anger."

"Often there were many more cards than I expected. Sometimes there were fewer than I had hoped. I was overwhelmed by the sheer volume of the life I had lived. Could it be possible that I had the time…to write each of these thousands, possibly millions, of cards? But each card confirmed this truth. Each was written in my own handwriting. Each signed with my signature. When I came to a file marked "Lustful Thoughts," I felt a chill run through my body. I pulled the file out only an inch, not willing to test its size, and drew out a card. I shuddered at its detailed contents. I felt so sick to think that such a moment had been recorded.

"Suddenly I felt an almost animal rage. One thought dominated my mind: "No one must ever see these cards! No one must ever see this room! I have to destroy them!" In an insane frenzy I yanked the file out. Its size didn't matter now. I had to empty and burn the cards. But as I took the file at one end and began pounding it on the floor, I could not dislodge a single card. I became desperate and pulled out a card, only to find it as strong as steel when I tried to tear it. Defeated and utterly helpless, I returned the file to its slot. Leaning my forehead against the wall, I let out a long self-pitying sigh…and then the tears came. I began to weep. Sobs so deep that the hurt started in my stomach and shook through me. I fell on my knees and cried. I cried out in shame, from the overwhelming shame of it all. The rows of file shelves swirled in my tear-filled eyes. No one must ever, ever know of this room. I must lock it up and hide the key.

"But then as I pushed away the tears I saw Him. No, please not Him. Not here. Oh, anyone but Jesus. I watched helplessly as He began to open the files and read the cards. I couldn't bear to watch His response. And in the moments I could bring myself to look at His face, I saw a sorrow deeper than my own. He seemed to intuitively go to the worst boxes. Why did He have to read every one? Finally He turned and looked at me from across the room. He looked at me with grace in His eyes. But this was a compassion that didn't anger me. I dropped my head, covered my face with my hands and began to cry again. He walked over and put His arm around me. He could have said so many things. But He didn't say a word. He just cried with me.

"Then He got up and walked back to the wall of files. Starting at one end of the room, He took out a file and, one by one, began to sign His name over mine on each card. "No!" I shouted, rushing to Him. All I could find to say was, "No, no," as I pulled the card from Him. His name shouldn't be on these cards. But there it was, written in red so rich, so dark, and so alive. The name of Jesus covered mine. It was written with His blood. He gently took the card back. He smiled a sad smile and continued to sign the cards. I don't think I'll ever understand how He did it so quickly, but the next instant it seemed I heard Him close the last file and walk back to my side. He placed His hand on my shoulder and said, "It is finished."

Walking in darkness and without a focus on relationship will leave you in shame. A personal relationship with the God of grace will set you free from shame!

Knowing Jesus
Lessons in the Gospel of John

Lesson Thirteen: John 8:12-59 "Show Me Something *Real*!"

Alice sat on a riverbank on a warm summer day, drowsily reading over her sister's shoulder, when she caught sight of a White Rabbit in a waistcoat running by her... The White Rabbit pulled out a pocket watch, exclaimed "I am late!" and popped down a rabbit hole. Alice followed the White Rabbit down the hole and came upon a great hallway lined with doors. She discovered a key on a nearby table, and opened a small door. Inside she gasped as she saw a beautiful garden! She started to cry when she realized she could not fit through the door. Only then did she notice a bottle marked "DRINK ME" and she did. She shrank down to the right size to enter the door but couldn't enter since the key was still on the table high above her head. She spied a cake marked "EAT ME" and obligingly she grew extremely large. Still held from the garden, she resumed crying. This time her giant tears formed a pool at her feet. She began to shrink into the pool that now appeared to become a sea, forcing her to tread water until she happened upon a Mouse. The Mouse and Alice made their way to the shore, where animals gathered on the bank. After a "Caucus Race," Alice told the listening animals of her cat, Dinah, and quickly found herself alone again... Confused by the bending of truth and the folds of reality, she was exasperated. "I need to see something **real**!" Alice exclaimed. Pleasant, fine, helpful, good... But when can I see something *real*!"

Who hasn't thought that? Who hasn't **awakened to the notion that something is very wrong down here**? People we **trust** turn out to be **untrustworthy. Ideas,** we AS A SOCIETY HELD, end up on the public **trash dump** as a new "truth" rolls into town. It has always seemed that there were **two worlds** – one mastering deception and one clamoring for truth. The crowds at the time of Jesus wanted to see more than a plotting and conniving leadership. They wanted to know if God was REAL, and how they could walk with Him (in spite of the leadership that seemed interested in controlling them for their own reasons!). They NEEDED to see a true relationship with God and they knew they didn't! Jesus gave them **FOUR STEPS to finding SOMETHING REAL**.

You see, what Alice needed was a REALITY CHECK. She needed a **pair of glasses** from the REAL WORLD to see what was going on was a fantasy. The truth is, SO DO WE!

Key Principle: Truth can only be grasped when I see the world through the Word of truth my Savior brought. I will not see the truth through glasses made by the world.

FOUR STEPS to finding SOMETHING REAL:

> **Step One - Understand the Real STANDARD**: I CANNOT BEGIN TO FOLLOW GOD UNTIL I CAN SEE THERE IS TRUTH, AND I NEED A GAUGE TO TELL WHAT IT IS (8:12-18).

John 8:12 Then Jesus again spoke to them, saying, "I am the Light of the world; he who follows Me will not walk in the darkness, but will have the Light of life." 13 So the Pharisees said to Him, "You are testifying about Yourself; Your testimony is not true." 14 Jesus answered and said to them, "Even if I testify about Myself, My testimony is true, for I know where I came from and where I am going; but you do not know where I come from or where I am going. 15 You judge according to the flesh; I am not judging anyone. 16 But even if I do judge, My judgment is true; for I am not alone in it, but I and the Father Who sent Me. 17 Even in your law it has been written that the testimony of two men is true. 18 I am He who testifies about Myself, and the Father Who sent Me testifies about Me."

- **Real Truth is found in the "lighted" place**: (Responding to the "set-up" trial of the adulteress woman). I show (turn the light onto) the truth - follow Me and you will see the REAL truth. (8:12). Your best rules of testimony and internal standards of truth are not relevant to the REAL TRUTH.

- **Real Truth comes from a "higher" place**: I know My origin (Truth comes from above – 8:14). Truth "fits" in Heaven (I know My destiny (8:14). I see beyond your world and commune with My Father in right choices and truth. My Father and I both tell you I offer the truth. (8:15-18).

Step Two - Identify the Real KEY: I CANNOT STAND IN BOTH WORLDS, I LEAVE ONE TO THE OTHER THROUGH THE DOOR JESUS UNLOCKED. (8:19-32)

John 8:19 So they were saying to Him, "Where is Your Father?" Jesus answered, "You know neither Me nor My Father; if you knew Me, you would know My Father also." 20 These words He spoke in the treasury, as He taught in the temple; and no one seized Him, because His hour had not yet come. 21 Then He said again to them, "I go away, and you will seek Me, and will die in your sin; where I am going, you cannot come." 22 So the Jews were saying, "Surely He will not kill Himself, will He, since He says, 'Where I am going, you cannot come'?" 23 And He was saying to them, "You are from below, I am from above; you are of this world, I am not of this world. 24 Therefore I said to you that you will die in your sins; for unless you believe that I am He, you will die in your sins." 25 So they were saying to Him, "Who are You?" Jesus said to them, "What have I been saying to you from the beginning? 26 I have many things to speak and to judge concerning you, but He Who sent Me is true; and the things which I heard from Him, these I speak to the world." 27 They did not realize that He had been speaking to them about the Father. 28 So Jesus said, "When you lift up the Son of Man, then you will know that I am He, and I do nothing on My own initiative, but I speak these things as the Father taught Me. 29 And He Who sent Me is with Me; He has not left Me alone, for I always do the things that are pleasing to Him." 30 As He spoke these things, many came to believe in Him.

- **Knowing Me is the key to knowing My Father.** You show your connection to Him by how you respond to Me. (8:19).
- **Knowing Me is the key to having your sin curse cured** - I am leaving you and you will die in your sin with no ability to come to where I am. (8:21).
- **Knowing Me is the key to changing your final destination**, for you and I come from different places – I am from above, you from the Earth. You cannot come where I am unless you believe I am Who I claim to be. (8:23-24).
- **Knowing Me is the key to understanding the Father's plan.** (Answering "Who are you?" Right question!) I am exactly Who I have been claiming to be, and rather than turn on you for your hardness, I will continue to report what My Father has told Me to say. (8:25-26). When you exalt Me, you will understand Who I am, and what I have done **in obedience** to My Father – I am on **His mission**, pleasing Him in all things. (8:28).
- **Knowing Me is the key to escaping the enemy's hold.** (To the new believers) If you cling to My teaching, you are true followers – and the truth you find in Me will set you free (from the world of the prince of deception!) (8:31).

Want to be free? We can be free of WORRY!

Statisticians at the University of Wisconsin have studied the things that we worry about. They found that the average individual's worries can be divided into 4 headings:

40% - things that never happened
  30% - things that happened that they can't change
  22% - petty worries
  8% - legitimate worries

Someone has said, Worry is wasting today's time to clutter up tomorrow's opportunities with yesterday's trouble.

A man was worrying all the time about everything. He was a chronic worrier. Then one day his friends saw him whistling. "Can that be our friend? No it can't be. Yes it is." They asked him, "What happened?" He said, "I'm paying a man to do my worrying for me."

"You mean you aren't worrying anymore?" "No whenever I'm inclined to worry, I just let him do it." "How much do you pay him?" "Two thousand dollars a week." "Wow! How can you afford that?" I can't. But that's his worry."

Step Three – Establish the Real ALLEGIANCE: I SHOW MY CITIZENSHIP BY MY LOYALTY.

John 8:33 They answered Him, "We are Abraham's descendants and have never yet been enslaved to anyone; how is it that You say, 'You will become free'?" 34 Jesus answered them, "Truly, truly, I say to you, everyone who commits sin is the slave of sin. 35 The slave does not remain in the house forever; the son does remain forever. 36 So if the Son makes you free, you will be free indeed. 37 I know that you are Abraham's descendants; yet you seek to kill Me, because My word has no place in you. 38 I speak the things which I have seen with My Father; therefore you also do the things which you heard from your father." 39 They answered and said to Him, "Abraham is our father." Jesus said to them, "If you are Abraham's children, do the deeds of Abraham. 40 But as it is, you are seeking to kill Me, a man Who has told you the truth, which I heard from God; this Abraham did not do. 41 You are doing the deeds of your father." They said to Him, "We were not born of fornication; we have one Father: God." 42 Jesus said to them, "If God were your Father, you would love Me, for I proceeded forth and have come from God, for I have not even come on My own initiative, but He sent Me. 43 Why do you not understand what I am saying? It is because you cannot hear My word. 44 You are of your father the devil, and you want to do the desires of your father. He was a murderer from the beginning, and does not stand in the truth because there is no truth in him. Whenever he speaks a lie, he speaks from his own nature, for he is a liar and the father of lies. 45 But because I speak the truth, you do not believe Me. 46 Which one of you convicts Me of sin? If I speak truth, why do you not believe Me? 47 He who is of God hears the words of God; for this reason you do not hear them, because you are not of God."

- **Your real allegiance is determined by your owner.** (Responding to "We are not slaves!") Live in **sin** and it is your **master** (8:33-34). People are enslaved, but they don't know it or believe it. It is obvious to those who see the world through the Word.
- **Your real allegiance to this world is a lost cause.** This sinful house will use you and discard you. It is a temporary set up, and has temporal objectives – and your good is not on the list! (8:35).
- **Your real allegiance can be felt in your hearts.** When I set you free – you have a permanent home as a son! You are the physical children of Abraham, but your heart is closed to Me. As a result *your real father* has whispered a lie in your ear and you plot to kill Me – and you *KNOW* it! (8:34-38).
- **Your real allegiance can be seen in your *character* viewed through your *choices*.** (Responding to Abraham is our father) If you were in heart Abraham's children, you would have his character. You are plotting against Me, and that shows you belong to another family! (8:40-41). (Responding to "We are actually children of God!") If you were children of God, you would

love Me as your Brother. You cannot understand what I am saying because you belong to your father, the Adversary, and you work for his purposes. He lied, plotted and took life from the beginning. His language is deception. You cannot find a lie in what I am saying, but you fight on because your heart is not open to God (8:42-47).

Step Four – Make the Real CHOICES: THERE IS A SPECIFIC WAY I CAN SEE WHERE I STAND – IT IS FOUND IN MY CHOICES.

John 8:48 The Jews answered and said to Him, "Do we not say rightly that You are a Samaritan and have a demon?" 49 Jesus answered, "I do not have a demon; but I honor My Father, and you dishonor Me. 50 But I do not seek My glory; there is One Who seeks and judges. 51 Truly, truly, I say to you, if anyone keeps My word he will never see death." 52 The Jews said to Him, "Now we know that You have a demon. Abraham died, and the prophets also; and You say, 'If anyone keeps My word, he will never taste of death.' 53 Surely You are not greater than our father Abraham, who died? The prophets died too; whom do You make Yourself out to be?" 54 Jesus answered, "If I glorify Myself, My glory is nothing; it is My Father Who glorifies Me, of Whom you say, 'He is our God'; 55 and you have not come to know Him, but I know Him; and if I say that I do not know Him, I will be a liar like you, but I do know Him and keep His word. 56 Your father Abraham rejoiced to see My day, and he saw it and was glad." 57 So the Jews said to Him, "You are not yet fifty years old, and have You seen Abraham?" 58 Jesus said to them, "Truly, truly, I say to you, before Abraham was born, I am." 59 Therefore they picked up stones to throw at Him, but Jesus hid Himself and went out of the temple.

- **You can choose to follow My Father by honoring ME**. (Responding to "You are a demon possessed Samaritan!") I absolutely represent My Father and yet you dishonor Me. I seek His glory – let Him be the judge! (8:49).

- **You can choose to have life by trusting My Word.** Follow My word and you will live forever! (8:50-51).
- **You can choose to follow REAL FAITH** (your father Abraham's heart) **and celebrate My presence.** (Responding to "Do you think You are better than Abraham?") If I sought to magnify Myself, it would be useless apart from My Father bestowing the honor upon Me. You don't know Him, but I do. If I said anything less, it would be a lie! Abraham looked forward to My day, and rejoiced! (8:54-56).
- **You can choose to accept what your eye cannot see.** (Responding to "How have you seen Abraham?") This is the simple truth: I am He Who was before – I am He Who existed before Abraham was ever born! (8:58).

Remember: Today's choices change tomorrow's destiny!

At a farmer's market in a little village there was a covey of quail walking in circles around a pole. They had strings attached to their legs, and they continued to walk around and around the pole hour after hour. A man came into the market and asked, "How much will you take for all of them?" He paid the owner the agreed upon price and then began to cut the strings off of their legs. "What are you doing?" the owner asked in unbelief? "**I'm setting them free,**" said the new owner. But in spite of the strings being cut giving the quail their freedom, they continued to walk around the pole in the same old circle. They didn't even realize that they were free and that they could go in a different direction. (source unknown)

I will not see the truth through glasses made by the world. Truth can only be grasped when I see the world through the Word of truth my Savior brought.

Lucado: "It happened too fast. One minute Barabbas was in his cell on death row playing tic-tac-toe on the dirt walls, and the next he was outside squinting his eyes at the bright sun. 'You're free to go.' Barabbas scratched his beard. 'What?' 'You're free, they took the Nazarene instead of you.'"

Knowing Jesus
Lessons in the Gospel of John

Lesson Fourteen: John 9:1-41 "I Can See Clearly Now!"

A man was sitting on the dock of a bay as the sunset over the water. The warmth of the sun beamed against his face as he smelled the salt air. The sounds of the seagulls surrounded him. The gentle breeze at his back flowed and began to cause the hairs on the back of his neck to stand at attention. He was relaxed and happy. A traveler came upon the man and observed that be barely moved, and almost never blinked. He asked the man what he was looking at. The man replied: "I can see a clear pallet of colors in this beautiful sunset. The colors are intense and warming." He spoke with the sound of deep satisfaction. Another man moved about on the dock as he was packing up his tackle into his fishing box and said, "And what is so remarkable, is they say MY FRIEND here is the blind man!"

The man reminds me that there are **many forms of blindness** in this world. Some of us were **stressed** this week, and saw no sunrises or sunsets. Some of us have been so work-dedicated for these past weeks we have not seen the changes in the faces of our children. Blindness comes in many ways…

Our story today is about a **blind man that was given sight**. What he saw at first was nothing more than the surroundings of the pool Jesus told him to go and wash in. **What he saw by the end of the story was the blindness that pervaded all the other people in his life.** He was healed physically when he washed, and was healed of spiritual blindness when he believed. Yet, sadly, he observed the blindness of those about him when he saw for the first time the **difference** between the **RELIGIOUS** (those who used their knowledge and training in God's rules to control others) and the **RIGHTEOUS** (The One

Who used the truth and power of God to free others). Real sight isn't physical; it is the ability to see the truth!

Most people **are blinded by false ideas they have come to accept as the truth**. The enemy has blinded the minds of men by deceiving them. They do not know the truth, and they believe the lies they have lived with for many years. They have **built a cell** and they live inside the cell. It is **not reality and truth**, but they do not know it is not.

Key Principle: Our blindness cannot be cured until we allow the Light of God's truth to displace the darkness of our deception!

SEVEN SCENES OF BLINDNESS:

Scene One: The blind man and the disciples of Jesus (9:1-7)

John 9:1-7 As He passed by, He saw a man blind from birth. 2 And His disciples asked Him, "Rabbi, who sinned, this man or his parents, that he would be born blind?" 3 Jesus answered, "It was neither that this man sinned, nor his parents; but it was so that the works of God might be displayed in him. 4 We must work the works of Him Who sent Me as long as it is day; night is coming when no one can work. 5 While I am in the world, I am the Light of the world." 6 When He had said this, He spat on the ground, and made clay of the spittle, and applied the clay to his eyes, 7 and said to him, "Go, wash in the pool of Siloam" (which is translated, Sent). So he went away and washed, and came back seeing.

In this scene, the disciples of Jesus were blinded by a false idea about God. They thought that trouble came to people only because God wanted to judge man. **Because of the teaching they were raised with, they could conceive of no**

other reason. They were blinded by a "**theological limitation.**" They could see only PART of what was going on, because they limited God to the options they knew about.

THEY THOUGHT THEY UNDERSTOOD ALL THE REASONS GOD DID WHAT GOD DID – and that was a blind spot in their lives.

Jesus sheds the light of **TRUTH** on the **half-truths and deceptions** by which men are ensnared. When the truth is exposed, false ideas can be seen for what they are – absurd twisting of God's intentions. We all live with limitations.

The blind man is bound by a limitation to his sight, the ignorant man by his limitation to know, the angry man by his limitation to control his mind – all facing limitations that hold them back. Sometimes limitations are brought on by a belief that is not correct, but is powerful enough to hold us back…

Wycliffe Bible translators Bob and Jan Smutherman were assigned to the Macuna people of southeast Colombia, South America. Progress was going well in putting the Bible into the Macuna language. The chief's son was engaged as the language helper. Each portion of the Scripture had to be checked and double-checked for meaning and clarity. After five years of labor, the Gospel of John was being finalized for publication. Gathered together to hear the Word of God, the tribe sat patiently. Beginning at John 9:1, the son read about Jesus' encounter with the man born blind. When he got to the verse where Jesus says that this man was born blind "in order that the works of God might be put on display," the old chief stood to his feet. Requiring silence by his uplifted right hand, he said, "We must stop killing our babies." To a people steeped in animism, the normal process was to take their deformed babies to a desolate place. There the babies were deserted and exposed until dead. Don't be blinded by judgment.

Scene Two: The blind man and the neighbors (9:8-12)

John 9:8-12 Therefore the neighbors, and those who previously saw him as a beggar, were saying, "Is not this the one who used to sit and beg?" 9 Others were saying, "This is he;" still others were saying, "No, but he is like him." He kept saying, "I am the one." 10 So they were saying to him, "How then were your eyes opened?" 11 He answered, "The man Who is called Jesus made clay, and anointed my eyes, and said to me, 'Go to Siloam and wash'; so I went away and washed, and I received sight." 12 They said to him, "Where is He?" He said, "I do not know."

In this scene, the neighbors were blinded by a false idea about possibilities. They believed that healing was not available to the forgotten and disenfranchised. They were caught in an "**experiential limitation**" – believing that only what they had experienced before was possible. They had no place for the God of the impossible!

When God opens the eyes of someone who has never before seen His inexhaustible ability to change the world, they discover a world of possibilities based on the power and majesty of the Creator! **THEY THOUGHT THEY KNEW ALL THE CHOICES THROUGH WHICH GOD WORKED** – and that was a blind spot to them.

For 51 years Bob Edens was blind. He couldn't see a thing. His world was a black hall of sounds and smells. He felt his way through five decades of darkness. And then, he could see. A skilled surgeon performed a complicated operation and, for the first time, Bob Edens had sight. He found it overwhelming. "I never would have dreamed that yellow is so…yellow," he exclaimed. "I don't have the words. I am amazed by yellow. But red is my favorite color. I just can't believe red. I can see the shape of the moon—and I like nothing better than seeing a jet plane flying across the sky leaving a vapor trail. And of course, sunrises and sunsets. And at night I look at the stars in the sky and the flashing light. You could never know how wonderful everything is."

For many a believer they *want* to see more happen, but they have been locked for too long in their own experiences. They haven't been challenged to see God as He truly is! **They serve a God in a box,** bound to their short understanding and deceived vision.

Scene Three: The healed man and the Pharisees (9:13-17)

8:13-17 They brought to the Pharisees the man who was formerly blind. 14 Now it was a Sabbath on the day when Jesus made the clay and opened his eyes. 15 Then the Pharisees also were asking him again how he received his sight. And he said to them, "He applied clay to my eyes, and I washed, and I see." 16 Therefore some of the Pharisees were saying, "This man is not from God, because He does not keep the Sabbath." But others were saying, "How can a man who is a sinner perform such signs?" And there was a division among them. 17 So they said to the blind man again, "What do you say about Him, since He opened your eyes?" And he said, "He is a prophet."

In this scene, the Pharisees were blinded by a false idea about their own authority. They believed that **their** understandings and traditions were the **truth**, though they were not direct expressions of the Word of God! They were caught in a "**tradition limitation.**" Any religious man or woman knows the temptation to make every teaching of their group equal to the absolute truth – but there is an inherent danger in doing so. **THEY THOUGHT THEY HAD INTERPRETED EVERY PRIORITY GOD CARED DEEPLY ABOUT** – and that was a blind spot to them.

We often do not see the most obvious lack in our logic!

Sherlock Holmes and Dr. Watson went on a camping trip. After a good meal and a bottle of wine, they lay down for the night and went to sleep. Some hours later, Holmes awoke and nudged his faithful friend. "Watson, look up and tell me what you see." Watson replied, "I see millions and millions of stars." "What does that tell you?" Watson pondered for a minute. "Astronomically, it tells me that there are millions of galaxies and potentially billions of planets. Astrologically, I observe that Saturn is in Leo. Horologically, I deduce that the time is approximately a quarter past three. Theologically, I can see that God is all-powerful and that we are small and insignificant. Meteorologically, I suspect that we will have a beautiful day tomorrow. Why, what does it tell you?" Holmes said, "Watson you idiot, someone has stolen our tent." Sometimes we are blind to what is going on right in our midst, and in a spiritual sense, we can be blind to what God is doing so well for us.

Scene Four: The Parents and the Pharisees (9:18-23)

9:18-23 The Jews then did not believe it of him, that he had been blind and had received sight, until they called the parents of the very one who had received his sight, 19 and questioned them, saying, "Is this your son, who you say was born blind? Then how does he now see?" 20 His parents answered them and said, "We know that this is our son, and that he was born blind; 21 but how he now sees, we do not know; or Who opened his eyes, we do not know. Ask him; he is of age, he will speak for himself." 22 His parents said this because they were afraid of the Jews; for the Jews had already agreed that if anyone confessed Him to be Christ, he was to be put out of the synagogue. 23 For this reason his parents said, "He is of age; ask him."

In this scene, the parents were blinded by fear of loss. They believed that the leaders would strip them of their position in the synagogue, and that would push them out of God's watch care. They would suffer in business and society, and God would not rescue them. They were caught in a "**fear limitation**", speaking things they didn't believe because they feared the consequences of taking a stand in the truth. **THEY THOUGHT THEY KNEW ALL THE WAYS TO GUARD WHAT THEY HAD GAINED** – and that was a blind spot to them.

Did you ever drive down a rainy road and lose the ability to see? Every foot you drive in blindness you fear because you cannot make out what is before you. You feel the weight of responsibility as a responsible driver, but you feel utterly unable to carry out the task.

A number of years ago in California, fierce winds from a dust storm triggered a massive freeway pileup. At least 14 people died and dozens more were injured as topsoil whipped by from 50 mile-per-hour winds reducing visibility to zero. The afternoon disaster left a three-mile trail of burning vehicles, some stacked on top of each other. The problem was, no one was able to see.

In another way, **the fear of loss is something that has held back thousands from the freedom of new life**. People are afraid that **Jesus will force them to give up things that are meaningful to them**, relationships they care about, fun they believe they cannot do without. How many are held back in the blindness that they cannot give up what they have for a commitment to Jesus?

Scene Five: The healed man and more Pharisees (9:24-34)

John 9:24-34 So a second time they called the man who had been blind, and said to him, "Give glory to God; we know that this man is a sinner." 25 He then answered,

"Whether He is a sinner, I do not know; one thing I do know, that though I was blind, now I see." 26 So they said to him, "What did He do to you? How did He open your eyes?" 27 He answered them, "I told you already and you did not listen; why do you want to hear it again? You do not want to become His disciples too, do you?" 28 They reviled him and said, "You are His disciple, but we are disciples of Moses. 29 We know that God has spoken to Moses, but as for this man, we do not know where He is from." 30 The man answered and said to them, "Well, here is an amazing thing, that you do not know where He is from, and yet He opened my eyes. 31 We know that God does not hear sinners; but if anyone is God-fearing and does His will, He hears him. 32 Since the beginning of time it has never been heard that anyone opened the eyes of a person born blind. 33 If this man were not from God, He could do nothing." 34 They answered him, "You were born entirely in sins, and are you teaching us?" So they put him out.

In this scene the Pharisees were blinded by pride. They believed they alone could tell truth from a lie. They suffered from an "**ego limitation.**" They saw their personal value in light of the control they could exercise on others. They felt strongly they were right, but that was a small part of the problem. The bigger part was that they were unwilling to face their own hearts and their own assumptions even when they no longer made sense! **THEY THOUGHT THEY HAD GREATER PERSONAL VALUE THAN OTHERS TO GOD** – and that was a blind spot in their lives.

Scene Six: The dismissed man and the Lord (9:35-39)

John 9:35-39 Jesus heard that they had put him out, and finding him, He said, "Do you believe in the Son of Man?" 36 He answered, "Who is He, Lord, that I may believe in Him?" 37 Jesus said to him, "You have both seen Him, and He is the one who is talking with you."

38 And he said, "Lord, I believe." And he worshiped Him. 39 And Jesus said, "For judgment I came into this world, so that those who do not see may see, and that those who see may become blind."

In this scene, the man who was physically healed experienced spiritual healing, when the TRUTH of the person of Jesus brought light into His heart. He was set free from the limitations as He embraced the truth that Jesus came to offer light to those who desired to see, but would pull the light back from those who chose to cling to darkness. **HE KNEW THAT JESUS TOLD THE TRUTH ABOUT HIMSELF, AND SHOWED THE TRUTH ABOUT LIFE** - and that became a lens through which he could see the world clearly!

Scene Seven: The Pharisees and the Lord (9:40-41)

John 9:40-41 Those of the Pharisees who were with Him heard these things and said to Him, "We are not blind too, are we?" 41 Jesus said to them, "If you were blind, you would have no sin; but since you say, 'We see,' your sin remains.

In the final scene, the Pharisees were blinded by stubbornness. They held their hearts back and believed that Jesus was not Who He claimed to be. They were held back by the "**unbelief limitation**" which offers the final damnation to any who continue to walk in it. THEY THOUGHT THEY KNEW THE TRUTH – but denying Him became the singular blind spot that led to their destruction!

Look at what we have seen more closely to really grasp the truth of this passage:

- **We can be blinded by believing we understand all God's options**, caught up in the theological limitations of our own understanding – cornering God into only the options we believe He can and should work in – but this blindness overstates our knowledge of God...

- **We can be blinded by the experiences we have shared**, believing that God will only do what He has seems to have done in our lives before – cornering our future into only the options of our past – but this blindness fails to allow God to do a NEW THING...

- **We can be blinded by the claims of our traditions**, believing that God's priorities are all limited by the traditions and customs of our group – pressing God into a mold of one of our members – but this is blindness that does not allow God to be bigger than our group...

- **We can be blinded by the fear that what we have we have attained and must preserve**, enslaved by the possibility that we will lose significance or happiness if our current hold loosens – pressing God's gifts to the edges of our lives and holding tightly to things earned at life's center – but this is a blind spot that will drive us forward without peace...

- **We can be blinded by the notion that we have an intrinsically higher value to God**, or place in His kingdom, believing that God has made us superior to others – pressing God to select our answers as the right ones in life – but this is the blindness of ego that keeps us too large to see God as He is...

Or we can be blinded by the stubbornness that seems to embrace the facts, but withholds its heart because of self-will – denying God is Who He claims to be in our lives – the Creator and maker of the rules – but this is a blind spot that leads to our self-inauguration as our own God – and our eternal death!

In each case, the central blindness of life can be defined as the WRONG VIEW ABOUT GOD HIMSELF! That is the source of real blindness!

That is why our blindness cannot be cured until we allow the Light of the world to displace the darkness of our deception with the light of God's truth!

We see when we believe the claims of the Savior – that HE is the Lord and Master worthy of our worship. When we see that, we see clearly.

Knowing Jesus
Lessons in the Gospel of John

Lesson Fifteen: John 10:1-21 "Ultimate Security"

The cocktail party was in full swing. The main floor of the marble floored mansion was filled with guests. The string quintet was playing, visitors were dancing. Ball gowns and tuxedos poured into the front door as a servant checked their invitations. The elegant and exciting were all joining the party. Little did the party host know a solitary man dressed in black, was suspending from a rope through the skylight of the second floor - breaking into his valuables in the wall safe.

There was more than one way into the house, but there is only one way to truly live securely in what the mansion provides.

The people who entered the ball properly came through the door, and had the blessing of their host. The man who entered through the skylight will leave in the police car. He got in the same house – a house filled with the sounds and smells of a party. Yet, he could not enjoy the things that were there. Even if he could, he could do so only for a short time, and then he would be taken out.

What was true of that thief is true of a great many religious people today. They walk amongst us as though they came into the party by the door. Yet, they will be discovered. Their enjoyment is not secure and their "part" is only a temporary one. God has an absolute security system.

Jesus offered these sayings before men who **seemed** to be at the party. In fact, they seemed to be **running** the party. They were Pharisees, and they were in control of local synagogues all over the Jewish world. The message of Jesus to them is the key principle I want us to focus on from this dialogue.

Key Principle: The Creator offers only one access point to the ultimate truth in life – Jesus Christ. You will not be coerced to accept that truth – but failure to do so will lead to terrible consequences. Believing a lie always does.

We pick up the middle of a discussion between Jesus and some offended Pharisees before a man some of their fellow Pharisees have tossed out of the synagogue because he would not deny Jesus' goodness after Jesus healed the man of blindness (which he had suffered all his life). Jesus told the Pharisees they were still living in sin because they claimed they could see spiritually, when in fact they could not.

> **A right way in:** People **try** to get into God's fold, but they don't want to enter the way God insists they must. The only true door is provided by the Father – any other approach is wrong.

John 10:1-2 Truly, truly, I say to you, he who does not enter by the door into the fold of the sheep, but climbs up some other way, he is a thief and a robber. 2 But he who enters by the door is a shepherd of the sheep.

The message needs to be clear on this point. The many prophets of the "All roads of goodness lead to God" are simply flat out wrong.

Where can I go to find out truth? Well, many would assume that it would be in the university system of our country.

If you attend this semester at San Francisco State University, you can take multiple courses in Asian History - Japanese and Chinese History. You can take courses in various cultures and their impact on the American experience. You can take courses in a variety of religious backgrounds. What you CANNOT find, is a single course that takes the Bible at its word and views the Biblical truth as the standard of truth. You will not see a posted "Ten Commandments" on any wall at the University.

You will however find a course in **Buddhism**. The course syllabus states: "Shakyamuni Buddha passed away around 486 BC at the age of eighty. Although he has left the world, the spirit of his kindness and compassion remains. The Buddha realized that he was not the first to become a Buddha. "There have been many Buddhas before me and will be many Buddhas in the future," the Buddha recalled to his disciples. "All living beings have the Buddha nature and can become Buddhas." For this reason, he taught the way to Buddhahood. The **two main goals** of Buddhism are getting to know **ourselves** and learning the **Buddha's teachings**. To know who we are, we need to understand that **we have two natures**. One is called our ordinary nature, which is made up of **unpleasant feelings** such as fear, anger, and jealousy. The other is our true nature, the part of us that is **pure, wise, and perfect**. In Buddhism, it is called the Buddha nature. The only difference between us and the Buddha is that we have not awakened to our true nature."

Note that the answer is not found outside of ourselves. It is NOT a connection to a Creator. Truth and happiness is found in you.

I recognize that in a pluralist society what I am saying is unpalatable. I simply argue that is what Jesus actually taught. His words, as recorded in the Gospels, became the basis of Christianity. Today, a majority of American Christians have developed a theological perspective that accepts both. More than 65% of Americans claim to be Christians, yet only 35% of Americans believe in a literal Hell. The idea that the text regulates what we think about God has been eroded by liberal theology and ignorance of the text itself. As a result, many who believe the Bible is GOOD, actually don't agree with what it says at all.

Jesus was exclusive in His teachings about the entry point to truth and to God – and He said that He is the Shepherd and the others were nothing more than thieves – entering the discussion on false pretenses.

You can choose to believe that He was wrong, or that the text did not accurately reflect His words – but in the end you must choose that at least the historic understanding of Christianity, and at most the teaching of Jesus Himself was wrong – and truth is found elsewhere. His words as recorded are NOT COMPATIBLE with Buddha.

There are TWO NATURES in the Bible, *but only in those who have found Jesus as their Savior* and have submitted their lives to Him and His teaching. The two natures are clearly described in a text where believers were acting like unbelievers:

1 Corinthians 3:1-3 And I, brethren, could not speak to you as to spiritual men, but as to men of flesh, as to infants in Christ. 2 I gave you milk to drink, not solid food; for you were not yet able to receive it. Indeed, even now you are not yet able, 3 for you are still fleshly. For since there is jealousy and strife among you, are you not fleshly, and are you not walking like mere men?

Paul established a contrast between **natural and spiritual natures** in Christians that were misbehaving. He shared the symptoms of their immaturity which included the inability to comprehend and live out spiritually discerned truths like unity. Since the text to this point has called them "brothers in Christ," we know they belonged to the group of "spiritual people." Paul offered comparisons between the natures: He said he wrote to them out of character of what they were - "not as to spiritual" because he felt forced to teach them **as if** they were not part of the spiritual group (i.e. alive to God), "but as to fleshly" (sarkinos) made of only the world materially and still alienated from God. He also claimed he was writing to them as to "infants" (nepios), addressing spiritual children. Though they had new birth in Christ they were inexcusably immature.

The Bible teaches that at the moment of salvation, **a new nature is poured in with the old nature**. The new nature is technically the renewal of the umbilical cord to God that was severed in the Garden of Eden, which the Bible referred to as DEATH. We are "made alive" (Ephesians 2:1) "having been dead in sin." From the moment we take in the new nature, a hostile coexistence begins.

One pastor wrote: "The old nature is older than the new nature, and the old nature continues to grow even though the Christian's new nature is also progressing. The old nature is at home in the world and continues to learn new things. This produces more conflicts with the new nature. The word carnal describes the bridge that the old nature builds to reach out into worldliness. Fulfilling the desires of the old nature produces attitudes and behaviors that are in opposition to God's will. It is not the new nature that responds to temptation; it is the old nature. It is not the new nature that doubts; it is the old nature. It is not the new nature that experiences fear and depression; it is the old nature. The new nature does not use profanity, but the old nature does. It is not the new but the old nature that envies, covets, lies, and steals. Many Christians have encountered periods of time when it seemed impossible to cope with life. The key is not so much trying to completely escape loneliness, depression, guilt, or discouragement as it is understanding that these things are produced by the old nature. By understanding this truth, the new nature can call on the Lord for support and prevent it from overwhelming his outlook on life."

The old adage helps make the point: "**Two natures live within: one is foul, the other blest; the one I love, the one I hate; the one I feed will dominate**."

The bottom line of what I am saying is that the teaching of the Bible is not the teaching of Buddha. The answer, says the Bible, is NOT FOUND WITHIN YOU. It is found by a reattachment to the God of the universe that was lost long ago in man's history. If Buddha was right, the answer is within you. If the Bible was right, the answer cannot be found within. **They are irreconcilably different and must be divorced.**

A right voice to heed: People must learn His voice and follow only that voice.

John 10:3-5 To him the doorkeeper opens, and the sheep hear his voice, and he calls his own sheep by name and leads them out. 4 When he puts forth all his own, he goes ahead of them, and the sheep follow him because they know his voice. 5 A stranger they simply will not follow, but will flee from him, because they do not know the voice of strangers.

This truth is akin to the one above, but emphasizes that **TRUTH CAN BE KNOWN, but the source must be THE ONE WHO KNOWS THE TRUTH.**

Wrong voices to shun: There are and were other voices, but they lead to prison.

Jesus used this metaphor of a sheepfold, but they didn't understand what He was saying.

John 10:7-10 So Jesus said to them again, "Truly, truly, I say to you, I am the door of the sheep. 8 All who came before Me are thieves and robbers, but the sheep did not hear them. 9 I am the door; if anyone enters through Me, he will be saved, and will go in and out and find pasture. 10 The thief comes only to steal and kill and destroy; I came that they may have life, and have it abundantly.

Some of the voices that have spoken a false view of faith have been found within the church. Don't let that seem strange, since this passage is rooted in that idea. Pharisees thought they could see (John 9:41) but Jesus called them **BLIND** because they were not only unseeing, but they thought they could see.

In the Bible, true spiritual blindness is rejecting relationship with the Living God for another religious plan based on a model you yourself have made.

Let me illustrate this by using an excerpt from Chuck Colson, the well-known Christian apologetics teacher, and founder of Prison Fellowship: "What is the Christian faith all about? One thing's for sure—it's about a lot more than your, or my, personal happiness. For many years, **Willow Creek Community Church** outside Chicago was the model that many evangelical churches sought to copy. Its growth, facilities and programs seemed to scream "**success**." That is, **until Willow Creek took a closer look**. The "look" was in the form of **two-year comprehensive study** that sought to determine which of its programs were helping it members to mature spiritually. The shocking answer was "not many." As pastor **Bill Hybels courageously put it**, some of their highest profile and best-funded programs didn't do much, if any, good. On the contrary, the things that people were "crying out for" went under-funded and starved of resources. **Hybels called the result of the study a "wake-up call."** In his words, "**We made a mistake.**" **In place of the "seeker friendly" program-centric model, Willow Creek seeks to instill in its members a desire to discover "what God is doing and how he's asking us to transform this planet."** Christian Smith of the University of North Carolina wouldn't be surprised at all at what Hybels and others have learned. Smith, a sociologist, has studied American Christianity in depth. In his book *Soul Searching: The Religious and Spiritual Life of American Teenagers*, Smith writes that the "de facto dominant religion" among American teenagers is what he calls "moral therapeutic deism." According to this "religion," God created and watches over the world but otherwise is only to be called upon to solve problems. All He requires is that people be nice and fair to each other, "as taught in the Bible and by most world religions." Not surprisingly, "the central goal of life is to be happy and to feel good about oneself." Smith notes that moral therapeutic deism is "more than a little visible" among conservative protestant teenagers. And it's not only teenagers. As theologian Albert Mohler has pointed out, what Smith describes is a belief "held by a large percentage of Americans." This kind of pablum is the logical outcome of reducing the entirety of the Christian faith to "Jesus and me." This Jesus does not challenge the way we see the world, much less how we live in it because He wants us to be happy; so He sanctions our desires."

Look at our text, and consider the Pharisee.

- He thought he could see, but he couldn't.
- He thought he was leading people to God, but he wasn't.
- He thought he was providing an important bridge to God from the world of the first century Jewish man or woman – but he wasn't.

His problem wasn't his **EFFORT**, his problem was he was **MISDIRECTED** about the answer. **He was even more dangerous because he taught as though he was right. False teaching isn't harmless** – it is **damning** when it claims to hold the path to life. Some teaching comes from within, but some comes from without as well.

Islam is a religion is named from an Arabic root word meaning "peace" and "submission." Islam teaches that one can only find peace in one's life by submitting to Almighty God (Allah) in heart, soul and deed as revealed in the Qur'an – their holy book. With well over one billion followers today (nearly 1/5 of the world population), it is usually associated with the Arabs of the Middle

East, though less than 10% of Muslims are in fact Arab. The people are followers of a god they call "Allah" - who they believe was the singular Creator of all – and who alone deserves love and worship. Muslims hold that any worship or prayer directed to anyone else is considered idolatry.

From the Qur'an we read (112:1-4): "In the name of Allah, the most beneficent, the most merciful, Say (O Muhammad): He is Allah, (the) One and Only. Allah, the Eternal, the Absolute. He begetteth not, nor was begotten, and there is none like unto him."

Lest anyone hear these words and think I am using them out of the context of Jesus, you should know that the Muslims of Nazareth hung them on the street leading to the *Church of the Annunciation of Mary* in Nazareth on December 24, 2008. They knew it was the time of Christmas pilgrimage, and they knew what the saying was for.

I am not trying to provoke anyone, I am making a simple point. Her Majesty Queen Noor of Jordan came to America after 9/11 to tell us that Islam's teachings are but one path to God, and they need not be seen as anything contradictory. Many nominal Christians, with little knowledge of either Islam or the Bible, were buying in. Clearly Oprah, who gave her the platform for her message, believed her. The bottom line isn't that they believe I am wrong in teaching the Gospels as truth – nor that I believe they are wrong because of my faith. **The bottom line is that it is deceptive to teach that one does not contradict the other.**

Jesus said: *God so loved the world that He gave His only begotten Son, that whoever believes in Him, will not perish, but have everlasting life. These words are both ABOUT Jesus and BY Jesus (John 3:16).*

If Islam is right, Jesus should not have received the worship of Thomas, who bowed to Him exclaiming, "My Lord and my God!" (John 20:28). I have no quarrel with them past this – we are irreconcilably different – and we are NOT saying the same thing. We are blind if we keep thinking they are really saying "sort of the same thing." They simply aren't. I can prove it. If I go to an Islamic country and teach the Bible, they will note that I am wrong. Period.

Jesus' claim that He was telling the truth and the others before Him (and for that matter that came after and did not agree with what He said) **were wrong, is at the heart of the Christian message.** You can't have a "nice guy" Jesus that gets along with everyone unless you reject the record of what He said and did. One wonders why such a person would call themselves a Christian at all.

> **A test to observe**: Trouble will come, but only in the true relationship will security be found.

John 10:11-18 I am the good shepherd; the good shepherd lays down His life for the sheep. 12 He who is a hired hand, and not a shepherd, who is not the owner of the sheep, sees the wolf coming, and leaves the sheep and flees, and the wolf snatches them and scatters them. 13 He flees because he is a hired hand and is not concerned about the sheep. 14 I am the good shepherd, and I know My own and My own know Me, 15 even as the Father knows Me and I know the Father; and I lay down My life for the sheep. 16 I have other sheep, which are not of this fold; I must bring them also, and they will hear My voice; and they will become one flock with one shepherd. 17 For this reason the Father loves Me, because I lay down My life so that I may take it again. 18 No one has taken it away from Me, but I lay it down on My own initiative. I have authority to lay it down, and I have authority to take it up again. This commandment I received from My Father.

Jesus wasn't simply a philanthropic philosopher. He knew that taking the stand He was taking was leading to a certain and painful end. The message of the New Testament is not that He was born and figured out through study that He was Messiah. Philippians 2:1ff explains that Jesus was very much alive in Heaven **BEFORE** He came to Earth, and had a conversation with His Father agreeing to come and do the work of saving men.

Jesus didn't just come to teach, heal and love. **He came with a full knowledge of the cost of coming.** He came as One Who would die on behalf of lost man. He argued that false teachers wanted something for themselves, and He wanted only to provide something for US – because it was the expressed will of His Father.

In the modern world of multi-culturalism and pluralist thinking, traveling philanthropists are now more the role models for modern religion. L. Ron Hubbard (1911-1986) the son of a naval officer, traveled extensively. The youngest Eagle Scout and an avid philosophy student, he met President Calvin Coolidge. He was introduced as a young man to the theories of psychoanalysis of Sigmund Freud. He began to study the human mind. He traveled to the Far East and learned extensively from eastern religions in India, China, Japan and the Philippines. He adopted many of the sage teachings of these places, and observed some "mystical events." He continued as a student at George Washington University as a scientist and engineering student. He led expeditions to the Caribbean and Puerto Rico. He studied ancient and primitive cultures and became an early pilot and navigator. He became a professional and prolific author. His popularity grew with over 300 novels. Another turning point came during his extensive travel and writing schedule when he, in 1937, felt he found the dynamic principle of all existence. He published it in *Excalibur* and later elaborated on it in the bestselling *Dianetics - The Modern*

Science of Mental Health. He left his career of writing to serve bravely in World War II. He is the founder of Scientology. He taught that he unlocked the secret to the mind, later believing that he discovered the very source of life, and the idea that you indeed have a past life. Today, his works are carefully studied by Scientology's followers. There is no question that L. Ron Hubbard was a brilliant and dedicated, hardworking student of humanity. **The issue is whether or not what he left us is the truth**.

Among Hollywood's elite, this pluralist hodgepodge of "seed picking" from various "truths" is a popular idea. It helps you be tolerant of people, and helps you seem well-rounded, well-educated – not extreme. Listen to the words of Jesus in light of that idea:

"I know the truth. I know My Father. I know My sheep." I KNOW. I am not on a journey, and I have not met the Chinese masters. I am at odds with the only sages of My time in My culture. I KNOW.

Doesn't sound so flexible, nor tolerant – don't you think? **Jesus wasn't interested in winning a popularity contest – that isn't what the truth is all about.** When He said: "I am the way, the truth, and the life – and no man comes to the Father, but by Me," he marked out His view of tolerance of other paths. He simply said they were not going to lead you to the right place, period.

> **A personal choice to make:** He is or is not telling the truth!

John 10:19-21 A division occurred again among the Jews because of these words. 20 Many of them were saying, "He has a demon and is insane. Why do you listen to Him?" 21 Others were saying, "These are not the sayings of one demon-possessed. A demon cannot open the eyes of the blind, can he?"

Everyone who has ever encountered the message of Jesus has been left with the same problem. If He was telling the truth, He must be acknowledged as God in human skin, and bowed before as the very incarnation of God Himself. God is One, yet has shown Himself in multiple personalities in Scripture in the same way "two become one flesh" in marriage. One in essence with His Father, He came claiming He alone was the TRUTH incarnate.

Your choice, and every other person on the face of the Earth's choice – is to believe Him, or think He was crazy. **The Gospel record is this: there is only one access point to the ultimate truth in life.** It is offered by the Creator by means of His Son. You will not be coerced to accept that truth – but failure to do so will lead to terrible consequences. **Believing a lie always does.**

In a large classroom, two men were called on to recite the Twenty-third Psalm. One was an orator trained in speech technique and drama. He repeated the psalm in a powerful way. When he finished, the audience cheered and asked for an encore that they might hear his wonderful voice again. Then the other man repeated the same words -- 'The Lord is my shepherd; I shall not want...' but when he finished, no sound came from the class. Instead, people sat in a mood of deep devotion and prayer. Then the first man stood to his feet. "I have a confession to make," he said. "The difference between what you have just heard from my friend, and what you heard from me is this: I know the Psalm, but my friend knows the Shepherd."

Knowing Jesus: Lessons in the Gospel of John (I)

Knowing Jesus
Lessons in the Gospel of John

Lesson Sixteen: John 10:22-42 "Hearing God"

There is an old story about a man who lived near a river that was dangerously rising in flood season. A radio report said that the river was going to rush up and flood the town and that all should evacuate. The man said, "I am religious, I pray, God will protect me!" As the waters rose, a man came by in a boat and shouted, "Hey you in there, come and get in my boat!" The man retorted, "I am religious, I pray, God will protect me!" A helicopter hovered above the house as the loudspeaker told the man to come out and be rescued. He called back "I am religious, I pray, God will take me to safety!' Well -- the man drowned. Standing in Heaven he asked, "**God, where were you?**" God said, "I sent you a radio report, a rescue boat and a helicopter... **what are you doing here?"**

Key Principle: God is speaking, but we may not have learned how to listen to Him!

Seven Problems Hearing God:

One. We want God to speak on our terms (when, where and how we want). *The Problem might be that I am not listening,* while accusing Him of silence, God is not holding out on me! The issue is my listening ear, not His voice speaking!

John 10:22 At that time the Feast of the Dedication took place at Jerusalem; 23 it was winter, and Jesus was walking in the temple in the portico of Solomon. 24 The Jews then gathered around Him, and were saying to Him, "How long will You keep us in suspense? If You are the Christ, tell us plainly." 25 Jesus answered them, "I told you, and you do not believe."

We have reversed the spelling of God from G-O-D to D-O-G: We think we can set the hoops and He will jump on our command. We say, "Here I am God, it is 11:00 AM on Sunday. I got here on time, and I brushed my teeth! I have football to watch later, so let's get to it. If you want to speak to me, I have done my part. I am here. Don't mess around now, you have got to make it obvious! Make sure it is right in the beginning of the sermon. Put your message to me right out there, 'cause I have had a busy week and I have a lot of other things to focus on. Make it memorable and simple. Make it funny and unforgettable!"

Maybe I am being too harsh. Perhaps your objection is more, "Well, **that was when Jesus was here, but I didn't live then!**" Does that mean the Heavens have become **silent** "declaring the glory of God"? Has the truth of what God is like become too obscure for you to pick out what He is like from the worlds that He has created?

Psalm 19:1 The heavens are telling of the glory of God; and their expanse is declaring the work of His hands. 2 Day to day pours forth speech, and night to night reveals knowledge. 3 There is no speech, nor are there words; their voice is not heard. 4 Their line has gone out through all the Earth, and their utterances to the end of the world. In them He has placed a tent for the sun, 5 which is as a bridegroom coming out of his chamber; it rejoices as a strong man to run his course. Its rising is from one end of the heavens and its circuit to the other end of them; and there is nothing hidden from its heat."

Two. We want to be able to draw any truth from what God says that takes us in a direction we already want to go! *The Problem might be what I draw from the truths God speaks.* His purpose is to tell His story and share Who He is with the Earth, but we place ourselves at the center of the story. The question isn't "How will this **help me**?" but rather, "How will this **reveal Him?**"

*John 10:25b ...the works that I do in My Father's name, these testify of **Me**.*

At long last, Jesus admitted to the real problem with the Bible and His message – it is not centered on ME. I am not the main character in this play. I don't like being second fiddle, I want to be the star. Yet, Jesus says HE is the star. His Father is the Author. I am to feel privileged to be in the show at all. I play the role He wants me to have. My time on the stage was chosen by Him, my role was set by Him. My performance is for an audience of those who have gone before, and the angelic world that watches the whole drama (while admittedly playing their roles).

*Hebrews 12: 1 Therefore, since we have **so great a cloud of witnesses** surrounding us, let us also **lay aside** every **encumbrance** and the **sin** which so easily entangles us, and let us **run with endurance** the race that is set before us, 2 fixing our **eyes on Jesus**, the Author and Perfecter of faith, Who for the joy set before Him endured the cross, despising the shame, and has sat down at the right hand of the throne of God. 3 For **consider Him Who** has **endured** such hostility by sinners against Himself, so **that you will not grow weary** and lose heart.*

Jesus ran a race ahead of us. His lap was exceedingly painful. His works showed Who He is, but also showed us the road that lay ahead for some of us – His children. It is not destined to all be an easy road.

A false Christian message is one that is centered on the BENEFITS of the walk, and not the race's primary purpose.

Three. We want Him to be committed to speak to us, even if we have expressed no commitment to Him! *The Problem might be that I don't really know Him at all.* God's voice won't be picked out by those who do not believe Him; they aren't who He does His talking to!

John 10:26 But you do not believe because you are not of My sheep. 27 My sheep hear My voice, and I know them, and they follow Me. \

God is under no obligation to speak to those who refuse to believe in Him, and those who refuse to accept that He is the very Creator of all things. If we want Him to speak only when we are in trouble, He is under no obligation to do so. He may do so in grace, but we cannot predict it. He has said that He will not leave us nor forsake us – but only to those who truly trust in Him.

*Hebrews 11: 1 Now faith is the assurance of things hoped for, the conviction of things not seen. 2 For by it the men of old gained approval. 3 By faith we understand that the worlds were prepared by the word of God, so that what is seen was not made out of things which are visible. .... 6 And without faith it is impossible to please Him, for **he who comes to God must believe that He is and that He is a rewarder of those who seek Him**.*

Four. We want Him to offer us the benefits of a relationship with Him (like communication, direction, and security) without the relational responsibilities on our end. God offers life and security to those who believe – **but we must BELIEVE**.

*John 10:28 ...and I give eternal life to them, and they will **never perish**; and **no one will snatch them** out of My hand. 29 My Father, Who has given them to Me, is* *greater than all; and no one is able to snatch them out of the Father's hand.*

2 Peter 1:2 Grace and peace be multiplied to you in the knowledge of God and of Jesus our Lord, 3 seeing that His divine power has granted to us everything pertaining to life and godliness, through the true knowledge of Him Who called us by His own glory and excellence. 4 For by these He has granted to us His precious and magnificent promises, so that by them you may become partakers of the divine nature, having escaped the corruption that is in the world by lust. 5 Now for this very reason also, applying all diligence, in your faith supply moral excellence, and in your moral excellence, knowledge, 6 and in your knowledge, self-control, and in your self-control, perseverance, and in your perseverance, godliness, 7 and in your godliness, brotherly kindness, and in your brotherly kindness, love. 8 For if these qualities are yours and are increasing, they render you neither useless nor unfruitful in the true knowledge of our Lord Jesus Christ. 9 For he who lacks these qualities is blind or short-sighted, having forgotten his purification from his former sins. 10 Therefore, brethren, be all the more diligent to make certain about His calling and choosing you; for as long as you practice these things, you will never stumble; 11 for in this way the entrance into the eternal kingdom of our Lord and Savior Jesus Christ will be abundantly supplied to you.

The assurance of your salvation, and the assurance that you will eternally have life is NOT rooted in the experience you had one day when you came to Jesus and asked Him to be your Savior. Your assurance is rooted in your growth. When you are stagnant, **God will withdraw your security and help you FEEL LOST even if you aren't. I offer no help to you. The words of Scripture ought always to lead us to holiness. Let no doctrine assure you when you do not walk with Jesus.** Be afraid and return. He is God, and there is no time to justify your self-will before Him. You must stop your rebellion and surrender anew. Do it now – **and do not reach into a theological bag of justifications of "back sliding." You know you aren't sure now, so why try to keep justifying sin?**

Five. We want Jesus to say things that fit my preconceived notions. *The Problem may be* that what He is saying forces you to reverse something you have believed. God may explain the truth but it is NOT what you were taught by someone you love. Maybe it has implications in Whom you serve and how you serve. Maybe it negates some deeply held understandings of your life.

*John 10:30 [Jesus said:] "I and the Father are one." 31 The Jews picked up **stones** again to stone Him. 32 Jesus answered them, "I showed you many good works from the Father; for which of them are you stoning Me?" 33 The Jews answered Him, "For a good work we do not stone You, but for **blasphemy**; and because You, being a man, **make Yourself out to be God.**"*

In our hearts we are willing to pick up stones when the Lord of the universe wants us to reach out and forgive someone we choose not to forgive. Maybe we don't want to KILL Jesus, but we wouldn't mind if He took His pointy stick somewhere else. We get equally obstinate when He tells us we **cannot participate in some activity** we really like to participate in, like when He tells us we **cannot eat or drink** something we really want to, even though we know we haven't gotten control over our eating and drinking and do not please Him. When He chooses **a different spouse** than the one we've been angling to get, when He **gives me talents** in areas other than the ones most noticed by others … the list goes on and on. I want what I want – but that isn't what Jesus said. **He said that He works as His Father wills, and He speaks the truth. We don't have to like it – it is no less the truth – even if it doesn't fit what I think He SHOULD be saying.**

Six. We want Jesus's words to take us where WE WANT TO GO. *The Problem might be* we don't want what He wants. They believed Messiah was a rescuer that would come to help THEM with THEIR perceived problems of foreign domination. Jesus came to say that Messiah came as the VERY ESSENCE of God (God poured into skin) and wanted to offer them a Kingdom that could only come if they were surrender within. They wanted **VICTORY** and God wanted **SURRENDER**!

*John 10:34 Jesus answered them, "Has it not been written in your Law, 'I SAID, YOU ARE GODS'? 35 If he called them gods, to whom the word of God came (and the Scripture cannot be broken), 36 do you say of Him, Whom the Father sanctified and sent into the world, 'You are blaspheming,' because I said, 'I am the Son of God'? 37 If I do not **do** the works of My Father, do not believe Me; 38 but if I do them, though you do not believe Me, believe the works, so that you may know and understand that the Father is in Me, and I in the Father." 39 Therefore they were seeking again to seize Him, and He eluded their grasp.*

While caught up in the words of Jesus that offended them, they were not able to defend against the logical argument He offered them from their own accepted and revered Scriptures.

His argument was:

- The law doesn't forbid My saying that I am in essence ONE with God.
- My works are consistent with the revelation of the Father that you say you revere.
- You have no legal cause to oppose Me – yet you know you do in your hearts!

Seven. We want unlimited chances to ignore His Word. *The Problem might be* that we argue until God withdraws what He has to say to offer it to another. We dare not presume that there will always be further chances, as our hearts harden each time we resist His truth!

Someone has said: Many people only want to date Jesus. They don't want to marry Him.

But I like what Wilbur Rees expressed: I'd like to buy $3.00 worth of God, please. Not enough to explode my soul or disturb my sleep, but just enough to equal a warm cup of milk or a snooze in the sunshine. I don't want enough of Him to make me love a black man or pick beets with a migrant. I want **ecstasy**, not **transformation**; I want the warmth of the **womb**, not a new **birth**. I want a **pound of the eternal in a paper sack**. I would like to buy $3.00 worth of God, please.

John 10:40 And He went away again beyond the Jordan to the place where John was first baptizing, and He was staying there. 41 Many came to Him and were saying, "While John performed no sign, yet everything John said about this man was true." 42 Many believed in Him there.

God is speaking, are you ready to listen to Him?

Knowing Jesus
Lessons in the Gospel of John

Lesson Seventeen: John 11:1- 46 "Night Vision"

The sentry marched in front of the gate, eyes ahead. Another guard watched the fence line from the tower, angling a spotlight along the fence anytime a rustle was heard from the bushes near the fence. It was difficult to see, and the light was the key to their defense. The commando unit pulled up to the edge of the jungle undetected. They could see ahead clearly with their night vision apparatus. They had the advantage, because they had "eyes" that could see what others could not.

Key Principle: Those who see the bigger picture of what God is doing live in the confidence that God made them and His plan is good.

Take a few minutes and look at John 11:1-46. The story is familiar – it is the death of Lazarus and the arrival of Jesus to Bethany. When you look closely, you see that Jesus had the ability to see what others did not and that made all the difference in what how He walked. He modeled something worth a second look!

People saw the sick man; **Jesus saw the opportunity for God's work** to be moved ahead. (The testimony of 11:45) Tragedy, disruption, detour are confidently handled when we believe that what God does apart from our poor choices is not our problem but our opportunity! (11:1-4) Jesus had using God's door of opportunity in mind.

John 11:1 Now a certain man was sick, Lazarus of Bethany, in the village of Mary and her sister Martha. 2 It was the Mary who anointed the Lord with ointment, and wiped His feet with her hair, whose brother Lazarus was sick. 3 So the sisters sent word to Him, saying, "Lord, behold, he whom You love is sick." 4 But when Jesus heard this, He said, "This sickness is not to end in death, but for the glory of God, so that the Son of God may be glorified by it."

His followers saw the danger, but **Jesus saw the clear direction from His Father** that now was the time to go. At times, waiting on the Lord will be interpreted by others as inaction. Yet, for one who truly seeks the Lord about what to do and when to do it, God will move them from the darkness to the light – and they will walk with confidence in that light. (11:5-10) Jesus had God's perspective in mind.

John 11:5 Now Jesus loved Martha and her sister and Lazarus. 6 So when He heard that he was sick, He then stayed two days longer in the place where He was. 7 Then after this He said to the disciples, "Let us go to Judea again." 8 The disciples said to Him, "Rabbi, the Jews were just now seeking to stone You, and are You going there again?" 9 Jesus answered, "Are there not twelve hours in the day? If anyone walks in the day, he does not stumble, because he sees the light of this world. 10 But if anyone walks in the night, he stumbles, because the light is not in him."

His followers took the little bit they heard and formed an opinion of what is "best" from it. **Jesus knew the situation, and understood that even His followers needed the troubles to help them see the truth.** Seek the Father about troubles. He has said that He will answer. When you know what He directs you to do, it is not a committee that decides – it is obedience to follow Him. (11:116) Jesus had God's testimony in mind.

John 11:11 This He said, and after that He said to them, "Our friend Lazarus has fallen asleep; but I go, so that I may awaken him out of sleep." 12 The disciples then said to Him, "Lord, if he has fallen asleep, he will recover." 13 Now Jesus had spoken of his death, but they thought that He was speaking of literal sleep. 14 So Jesus then said to them plainly, "Lazarus is dead, 15 and I am glad for your sakes that I was not there, so that you may believe; but let us go to him." 16 Therefore Thomas, who is called Didymus, said to his fellow disciples, "Let us also go, so that we may die with Him."

In pain we lament the trouble. We believe that God didn't really want it to happen, because we think we understand the impact our trouble has on the universe – because we hurt over it.

Yet, **Jesus saw the big picture of the Father at work** – both then and in the future. It is that confidence that helps a believer walk through trouble, When I know the bigger plan in play, I can walk in faith despite the troubles without losing my grip. (11:17-37) Jesus had God's plan in mind.

John 11:17 So when Jesus came, He found that he had already been in the tomb four days. 18 Now Bethany was near Jerusalem, about two miles off; 19 and many of the Jews had come to Martha and Mary, to console them concerning their brother. 20 Martha therefore, when she heard that Jesus was coming, went to meet Him, but Mary stayed at the house. 21 Martha then said to Jesus, "Lord, if You had been here, my brother would not have died. 22 Even now I know that whatever You ask of God, God will give You." 23 Jesus said to her, "Your brother will rise again." 24 Martha said to Him, "I know that he will rise again in the resurrection on the last day." 25 Jesus said to her, "I am the resurrection and the life; he who believes in Me will live even if he dies, 26 and everyone who lives and believes in Me will never die. Do you believe this?" 27 She said to Him, "Yes, Lord; I have believed that You are the Christ, the Son of God, even He Who comes into the world." 28 When she had said this, she went away and called Mary her sister, saying secretly, "The Teacher is here and is calling for you." 29 And when she heard it, she got up quickly and was coming to Him. 30 Now Jesus had not yet come into the village, but was still in the place where Martha met Him. 31 Then the Jews who were with her in the house, and consoling her, when they saw that Mary got up quickly and went out, they followed her, supposing that she was going to the tomb to weep there. 32 Therefore, when Mary came where Jesus was, she saw Him, and fell at His feet, saying to Him, "Lord, if You had been here, my brother would not have died." 33 When Jesus therefore saw her weeping, and the Jews who came with her also weeping, He was deeply moved in spirit and was troubled, 34 and said, "Where have you laid him?" They said to Him, "Lord, come and see." 35 Jesus wept.

The people saw the weeping Jesus, asking that the tomb be opened. Martha thought she knew the situation better than Jesus and advised Jesus not to open the tomb. We often think we need to inform the Savior and give Him advice. Jesus knew that God heard Him in the conversation about this moment they ALREADY HAD. That was the secret.

Jesus had obedience to God's direction in mind.

John 11:38 So Jesus, again being deeply moved within, came to the tomb. Now it was a cave, and a stone was lying against it. 39 Jesus said, "Remove the stone." Martha, the sister of the deceased, said to Him, "Lord, by this time there will be a stench, for he has been dead four days." 40 Jesus said to her, "Did I not say to you that if you believe, you will see the glory of God?" 41 So they removed the stone. Then Jesus raised His eyes, and said, "Father, I thank You that You have heard Me. 42 I knew that You always hear Me; but because of the people standing around I said it, so that they may believe that You sent Me." 43 When He had said these things, He cried out with a loud voice, "Lazarus, come forth." 44 The man who had died came forth, bound hand and foot with wrappings, and his face was wrapped around with a cloth. Jesus said to them, "Unbind him, and let him go." 45 Therefore many of the Jews who came to Mary, and saw what He had done, believed in Him. 46 But some of them went to the

Pharisees and told them the things which Jesus had done.

Because of these five things, Jesus could see what others around Him could NOT see.

So, what is the night vision that Jesus had?

- He saw each day's troubles as God's open door of opportunity to see things from God's perspective, because He spent time with His Father.
- He sought Him about responses to pain and trouble
- He looked for how the pain and trouble could be used to further the testimony of His heavenly Father's greatness.
- He looked for ways to expose the plan and purpose of God in daily life.
- He walked in obedience to His Father's direction.

They felt the pain, and groped in darkness.

Jesus felt the pain and pulled Himself into the light of His Father's direction.

They accessed their experience and tried to tell God how it should be.

Jesus listened to His Father and saw how it must be.

They tried to explain away how a good and loving Father could purpose such PAIN in their lives.

Jesus accepted His Father's knowledge as superior and sought to hear the voice of His Father concerning the pain and follow the Father's plan to bring glory to Him.

Jesus possessed the night vision goggles that brought clear vision when others saw darkness... and we can possess them too!

Those who see the bigger picture of what God is doing live in the present with a firm confidence. The confidence is not in the situation, nor in this life, but in the God that made them and His good plan.

Knowing Jesus
Lessons in the Gospel of John

Lesson Eighteen: John 11:47-57 "The Titanic Choice"

When the Titanic embarked on her maiden voyage in early April, 1912, the world was filled with pride and joy. In a few short days, jubilation turned to horror and grief. One fascinating part of this historic tale was recorded by a few of the 705 survivors of the original 2228 people on board. The diaries of the survivors illustrated vividly that there are really three kinds of people – confused and fearful, manipulative and pushy, and those who followed the Captain's commands. It is always this way – there are three kinds of people.

The following was written by Jack Jordan newspaper editor recording the events of April 3, 1974: "An uneasiness nagged at me as I checked over proofs for the next day's paper. It was Wednesday, April 3, 1974 about 4 o'clock on a gray afternoon. More than 100 tornadoes had been sighted to the southwest. We had such warnings before - but the twisters had always missed Xenia, Ohio. Suddenly the radio crackled: '**Tornado**! Southwest of town, expected in six minutes.' I leapt from desk and hurried out into our office which faces the main downtown street. Police shouted "Take Cover!" through bullhorns. Already white-faced shoppers and business people were streaming into our new annex building for the protection of its steel beam and thick concrete construction. Suddenly an ominous green darkened the street. A rumbling roar like a thousand freight trains crossing the ceiling filled the building with a grinding thunder. Our front doors flew open, I rushed to close them and found myself looking up into a black swirling sea of debris and giant trees. I fought my way back and threw myself down on the stairs among the other praying and sobbing people. Soon an eerie stillness filled the air. The monster had passed. My family and home were two miles away. I ran to my convertible, its windows sucked out. I sat in broken glass and drove down the street. There were no more house-lined streets - just mountains of debris and dazed and confused people wandering around. After making sure that my family was okay, I returned to the newspaper office. The tornado had bulldozed a seven mile path half a mile wide right through Xenia, Ohio. Thirty-three men, women, and children were dead. Almost half of Xenia's buildings were destroyed. Nearly 10,000 people were homeless. Six of nine schools were smashed. Nine churches, and 180 stores and businesses were destroyed. In the coming months the city would pull together and begin to rebuild houses, businesses, churches, schools, and lives. One afternoon, seven months later, I walked downtown and remembered the houses that owners had spray-painted with the words 'Oh God, why us?' and 'Only God knows.' And I remember what Dick Pope, a minister, said at an Easter celebration just eleven days after the tornado. 'For the first time people are really going to understand what resurrection is about. **You have to realize that Christ was even more effective after the resurrection than before**. This storm can be a turning point for this town. The Christian faith does not promise that we will not have suffering, but it **should create the character in us that can face it and know how to use it.**' I want to talk to you today about our lives and how we deal with it when disaster comes into our lives. *WHAT KIND OF PERSON ARE YOU?* Whether it is a natural disaster like a tornado, or a health disaster like cancer, whether it is relationship disasters like a broken marriage, whatever the disaster is... How do you respond to the different types of people there are?" (Pastor James Chandler, Peebles Church of Christ, Peebles, Ohio)

Go back two thousand years and we can observe the same truth that not everyone handles tragedies in life the same way. John 11:1-46 revealed that after Jesus raised Lazarus, He left Bethany for the village of Ephraim on the edge of the wilderness. **People were increasingly following** because of the Lazarus miracle, and word soon got back to the temple court…

They weren't interested in FOLLOWING. They had CONTROL on their minds…

Key Principle: Only those who choose to follow the Master get the true benefits of His power, presence and purpose.

THREE KINDS OF PEOPLE

There is an old adage that there are three kinds of people: The kind that **MAKE** things happen, the kind that **WATCH** things happen, and the kind that **WONDER WHAT HAPPENED**. I believe the passage today shows three kinds of people, and they are similar to these three I just mentioned.

TYPE 1: Wonder what is happening:

People who live in **FEAR** of any agenda… and can easily become manipulated by the second group.. Pharisees saw a THREAT. Pharisees said **inaction** would lead to **loss** of the nation. They felt the **need** to protect what was not theirs – the **nation** that was God's own. When we take on the responsibilities we don't have, we create a sense of panic and search for resolutions we are forcing on ourselves.

John 11:47 Therefore the chief priests and the Pharisees convened a council, and were saying, "What are we doing? For this man is performing many signs. 48 If we let Him go on like this, all men will believe in Him, and the Romans will come and take away both our place and our nation."

The people who were led by FEAR made a series of bad assumptions:

They thought <u>together</u> they could solve the problem. It is amazing to see how often people who are **lost** will **band together** when none of them have any idea how to get out of the situation. Standing wet in a vast pool of ignorance is somehow more comforting than standing alone in the deserted place. It is as though they were confronted with a CALCULUS problem and they were all DRAMA majors. No one was at all sure how to solve the problem, but the room was crowded with people who (most likely for some point of self-interest) were pushing for an immediate solution.

Beware of those who make you feel panic so they can get you to decide on a solution that no one can be certain will help. Fear is an excellent motivator for poor decision processes. Remember, the **difference between MOTIVATION and MANIPULATION is the motive** in the leadership. If the motive of national leadership is preservation of power (as in these verses) and not primarily the benefit of the people they serve – the decision will not be a good one. They could SPIN that they were concerned for the people, but a broader history of these men demonstrates otherwise. The right answer can only be found when the right picture is presented to the decision makers, and they work on an honest plan that includes facing all the facts (including their own prejudices).

They thought they were asking the right questions. "What are WE DOING?" wasn't the only question they should have been asking. **They should have desired to know what ACTUALLY HAPPENED at Bethany, where Lazarus was raised.** The debate should have raged in that room as to HOW a man they called a **demoniac** (Jesus) was able to cause his friend to cross through the veil from death to life! No one was asking the right questions.

They thought everything was related to what <u>THEY</u> could and would do. As men who governed a people, you would think they would have understood that **they couldn't simply move the people's opinions around like parliamentary furniture**. They seemed to believe they could change everything by THEIR actions. **It is firmly within the**

nature of those who govern to get caught up on the wrong questions and forget the obvious ones. Instead of trying to look at what Jesus was doing, those in charge were busy trying to decide how they could keep control of the situation.

They thought they had the power to stop HIM. Think about that assumption. He was able to bring a man back from the dead, but they could... do what... KILL HIM? That doesn't seem like the best solution.

It reminds me of when I used to watch Batman back when I was a kid. I could never figure out why the bad guy would **catch Batman and Robin** and then hatch an **elaborate plot to kill them** in the slowest and least efficient way. Considering the number of times the "dynamic duo" got loose from such snares, it seemed stupid that the next guy did the same thing. Why didn't they get it? Well, that was only television...

Our story is from history, and they didn't get it either. Remember, it is in the nature of the halls of power to fail to see the limitations of power. As such, they believed they could shut down a man who had the power over death by killing Him. In retrospect, **none of them would argue for this position today**.

They thought they could shape what PEOPLE would believe. If we let Him go on, everyone will believe in Him, was their claim. A bit exaggerated when they weren't exactly at the center of civilization to begin with. What is more, Jesus' relative popularity was by no means assured when people really heard the message that He preached. He spoke often of commitment and assured the people that His follower's journey was the road less traveled. Be that as it may, they thought they could SPIN beliefs and shut down His growth by getting to Jesus with a silencer. History has a way of allowing the truth to eventually come out... there have been few who could be silenced that offered such a strong message.

They thought they could stop what world powers would do to them. The classic miscalculation is the one that says, "If we don't do anything wrong, this world's dominating and merciless dictator won't hurt us." Take the desire to control seriously in people that express world domination as their goal. When any group, be they ancient Roman or modern Near Eastern religions, says they intend to take control by force – don't expect them to play fair or nice. I am still wondering why the world excuses world leaders who spew out hatred in the UN of the country that paid the light bill.

They thought they HAD a nation, though clearly they felt it was out of control. On the one hand they were trying to protect what they had, and on the other hand they expressed no real confidence that they could control it internally or externally. At the end of the day, people in the seat of power often hold less power than they believe. When they realize that truth, they often try to leverage more control through fear.

When Hetty Green died on July 3, 1916, she passed into history as an American businesswoman, remarkable for her legendary frugality (read the word CHEAP) during the Gilded Age, as well as for being the first American woman to make a substantial impact on Wall Street. Green made much of her business at the offices of the Seaboard National Bank in New York, surrounded by trunks and suitcases full of her papers; she did not want to pay rent for an office. Her frugality extended to family life. Her son Ned broke his leg as a child, and Hetty tried to have him admitted in a hospital charity ward. When she was recognized, she stormed away vowing to treat the wounds herself. The leg contracted gangrene and had to be amputated—he ended up with a cork prosthesis. When her children left home, Green moved repeatedly among small apartments in Brooklyn Heights and Hoboken, New Jersey, mainly to avoid establishing a residence permanent enough to attract the attention of tax officials in any state. In her old age she refused an operation because it cost $150. She suffered many strokes and had to rely on a wheelchair. Hetty Green died at age 81 in New York City in an apartment that had heat she would not use because of the cost of utilities. She lived, by all accounts, an eccentric life. Many believed she lived in FEAR of LOSS. (*WIKIPEDIA*)

Take a moment and look at the CONTRAST to the <u>CONTROL</u> of Jesus expressed in John 11:4 But when Jesus heard this, He said, "This sickness is not to end in death, but for the glory of God, so that the Son of God may be glorified by it." In Him you see no FEAR, nor CONFUSION.

TYPE 2: Make things happen:

Not everyone is moved by FEAR. Some people are always looking at every situation by the angles of how it will help them. These people live to **MANIPULATE** every agenda…The High Priest saw an **OPPORTUNITY**. The High Priest said **corruption** would lead to **solution.** He felt the **right** to take what was not his – the **Son** that was God's own.

When we aren't tied to the moral truths of God's Word, we track into wrong territory.

John 11:49 But one of them, Caiaphas, who was high priest that year, said to them, "You know nothing at all, 50 nor do you take into account that it is expedient for you that one man die for the people, and that the whole nation not perish."

There are **two critical assumptions that manipulators make:**

They think their temporary title makes them smarter than everyone else (11:49). Caiaphas was the High Priest on that particular year. He was of the household of Hannan, one of three important households that were vying for the power over the Jerusalem Temple and its lucrative markets. He thought he was smart, but he is not remembered well in history. It is clear that in the NT he comes off badly. Yet, the same is true in Jewish literature. In the Mishnah, Parah 3:5 it refers to him as Ha-Koph (**the monkey**), a play on his name for opposing a movement among the Hasidim of his day. One day on top of the world, the next day they are calling you "monkey boy" at your back.

Just remember, when you get an important title you are either a LORD or a SERVANT. I can so easily get caught up being important – can't you? How many so called "public servants" are found guilty in crimes that are... well, really STUPID. Do they really think that picking up a prostitute is going to go unnoticed by the paparazzi? I wonder about people...Yet they think the rules don't apply to them and that they truly are smarter than others.

- It reminds me of the cartoon I saw of a king standing in front of his throne with a long face. In the first frame he is looking forlorn at the floor. He said: "Some of my subjects are saying that I am power hungry..." Frame two: He looks up and says to his adviser, "**Have them executed**."

- My other cartoon favorite on power is the one that showed a dad talking to his child :"Surely you can grow up to be the **President**. But for REAL POWER consider becoming a **LOBBYIST**!"

They think their might makes them right about moral judgments that affect everyone else (11:50). Right is determined by what God says. It is not cultural or subjective – in spite of the fact that both are being screamed at us every day.

Lon Grammer claimed some impressive credentials when he transferred to Yale from Cuesta Community College in San Luis Obispo, Calif., two years ago, including a 3.9 grade point average. He did well at Yale, too, playing rugby while earning a B average. But a bare month before he was to graduate with a degree in political science, Yale expelled the 25-year-old and charged him with taking $61,475 under false pretenses. School officials say he lied about his GPA and forged recommendations from nonexistent teachers. He was arraigned on larceny charges. In a TV interview, he pleaded that his actions were no worse than what happens every day when people lie on resumes. (*U.S News & World Report*, April 24, 1995, p. 20)

A pastor I know, Stephey Belynskyj, starts [Bible] class with a jar full of beans. He asks his students to guess **how many beans are in the jar**, and on a big pad of paper writes down their **estimates**. Then, next to those estimates, he helps them make another list: their **favorite songs**. When the lists are complete, he **reveals the actual number of beans** in the jar. The whole class looks over their guesses, to see **which estimate was closest to being right**. Belynskyj then turns to the list of favorite songs. "**And which one of these is closest to being right**?" he asks. The students protest **that there is no "right answer,"** a person's favorite song is purely a matter of taste. Belynskyj, who holds a Ph.D. in philosophy asks, "**When you decide what to believe in terms of your faith, is that more like guessing the number of beans, or more like choosing your favorite song**?" "Always," Belynskyj says, "from old as well as young, he gets the same answer: **Choosing one's faith is more like choosing a favorite song.**" When Belynskyj told me this, it took my breath away. "After they say that, what do you do?" I asked him. "Well," smiled Belynskyj, "I try to show them the error. Sadly, many don't believe there can be one! (Adapted from Tim Stafford / brackets mine, *Christianity Today*, September 14, 1992, p. 36)

TYPE 3: Follow the Leader:

People who live for **HIS** agenda...**Narrator saw God's PLAN**. The narrator said that Jesus' death covered both Israel and others afar off.

John 11:51 Now he did not say this on his own initiative, but being high priest that year, he prophesied that Jesus was going to die for the nation, 52 and not for the nation only, but in order that He might also gather together into one the children of God who are scattered abroad.

Look at John's **three assumptions as a follower:**

- **God was at work**: The High Priest may have spoken the words, but God was doing something bigger than that man ever perceived.
- **Jesus wasn't just killed BY them, but FOR them**: They may have been plotting, but God's plan was what was in play!
- **The Agenda was HUGE**: God was going to use this work to change the world!

2 Corinthians 5:14 For the love of Christ controls us, having concluded this, that one died for all, therefore all died; 15 and He died for all, so that they who live might no longer live for themselves, but for Him who died and rose again on their behalf. 16 Therefore from now on we recognize no one according to the flesh; even though we have known Christ according to the flesh, yet now we know Him in this way no longer. 17 Therefore if anyone is in Christ, he is a new creature; the old things passed away; behold, new things have come. 18 Now all these things are from God, who reconciled us to Himself through Christ and gave us the ministry of reconciliation, 19 namely, that God was in Christ reconciling the world to Himself, not counting their trespasses against them, and He has committed to us the word of reconciliation.

THERE ARE THREE TYPES OF PEOPLE... WHICH ARE YOU?

MAYBE you should consider the RESULTS before you answer:

- **Manipulators end up on THEIR agenda, with great plans and God withdrawn** – and as a result they lost His blessing! They lost the blessings that would have come from continued time with Jesus.

Note in *John 11:53 So from that day on they planned together to kill Him. 54 Therefore Jesus no longer continued to walk publicly among the Jews.*

- **Followers commit to HIS agenda, and as a result they got His presence and continued direction!**

John 11:44b: ...but went away from there to the country near the wilderness, into a city called Ephraim; and there He stayed with the disciples.

- **Wonderers continue to walk in confusion…**

John 11:55 Now the Passover of the Jews was near, and many went up to Jerusalem out of the country before the Passover to purify themselves. 56 So they were seeking for Jesus, and were saying to one another as they stood in the temple, "What do you think; that He will not come to the feast at all?" 57 Now the chief priests and the Pharisees had given orders that if anyone knew where He was, he was to report it, so that they might seize Him.

Dad was busy watching TV … It was an important football game. The little girl kept bothering him wanting to go get a treat at the corner store (a practice they routinely performed). Finally, frustrated at her persistence at this particular time, he reached over and picked up a magazine and quickly thumbing through it found a picture of the world. Taking his scissors, he cut the picture out, then cut it into a number of much smaller pieces. Handing the pieces to the little girl, along with a roll of scotch tape he said, "Put this together, and when you have it looking like the world again, I promise you we'll go get that candy bar." Thinking he had pulled a good one and could watch the rest of the game in peace, he sat back down and got totally absorbed. After about seven or eight minutes the little girl came back in holding up a picture of the world all taped back together nice and neatly. He couldn't believe it! (HOW? – he knew he couldn't have done it so quickly.) "Well daddy, **I noticed on the back of the picture when you were cutting it up there was a picture of Jesus being put onto the cross. And when I put Him in the right place, the world all came back together.**" As he turned off the TV and he and his little girl headed out the door, he recalled those words – **"When you put Jesus in the right place, the world all comes back together."**

Only those who choose to follow the Master – to put His work at the CENTER - get the true benefits of His power, presence and purpose. Life won't make sense any other way.

Volume II of Knowing Jesus completes our study of the Gospel of John.

Other volumes in the series through the Bible are available through amazon.com and can be found by searching for:

"Dr. Randall D. Smith"

Free teaching resources are also available at:

www.randalldsmith.com

www.ingramcontent.com/pod-product-compliance
Lightning Source LLC
Chambersburg PA
CBHW071458040426
42444CB00008B/1391